TELEPHONE TERRORISM

The Story of Robocalls and the TCPA

Dennis Brown

ALSO BY THE AUTHOR

Who Voted for the Hologram?
A Gruff Guidebook to the Presidential Libraries

How Not to Run for Pope

Copyright © 2019 Dennis Brown. All rights reserved.

No part of this publication may be reproduced, distributed or transmitted in any form or by any means, or stored in a database or retrieval system, without the prior written permission of the author.

First Paperback Edition, October 2019

ISBN # 9781697693812

CONTENTS

Introduction 3
Prologue: Attack of the Trash Calls 6
1. Ernest Writes a Law 11
2. The TCPA: Trespassing Callers Punished Appropriately..... 23
3. The Courts Have Their Say 31
4. The Crackdown of 2003 43
5. Political Robocalls: One More Reason Not to Vote 53
6. Long Distance Panhandlers 67
7. Debt Collectors: The World Champions of Robocalling 78
8. Turning Robocalls (and Faxes) into Riches 96
9. The Scam-Based Economy 113
10. Confusion All Around 131
11. The Crisis Enters Its 4th Decade 150
Epilogue: Taking Out the Trash 157
Notes 162
Appendix: The Telephone Consumer Protection Act 183

INTRODUCTION

If you own a telephone, you are certainly familiar with robocalls. These are the automated messages that come to us many times each week, usually asking us to press "1" to speak to an agent about an exciting opportunity. In an America where political discord is constantly in the spotlight, robocalls provide a rare point of unity: everyone despises them.

The robocall epidemic has become a frequent theme of alarming news stories. These reports tell us that unwanted automated calls grew by more than half in 2018 and will soon account for the bulk of telephone traffic in the United States. Spam texting is on the rise as well. The nuisance calls and texts are projected to increase until cellular networks are totally overwhelmed, and we will have to revert to loud shouting as the only means of long distance verbal communication. Then there will undoubtedly be spam shouters standing outside our home and office windows with megaphones, offering to lower our interest rates if we yell our credit card numbers back to them.

There is an enormous amount of arrogance embodied in an automated call, especially when it comes from a self-interested party like a telemarketer, a bill collector, or a politician. Somebody wants a chunk of our time and attention, but isn't willing to sacrifice any of his own. Perhaps this is why these calls infuriate people so much.

But this type of telephone technology can be used for beneficial purposes too. A recorded message might be sent by our child's school, telling us that classes have been cancelled because an evil clown was sighted in the area. A robocall can come from our grocery store, informing us that the cereal we bought and consumed last summer contained an undeclared nut allergen, and that we are probably dead now. Or we might receive an automated text from our airline, notifying us that the flight we are waiting for at Gate A1 will now be departing from Gate R99 in two minutes. If unsolicited spam calls cause us to stop answering our phones, we will miss important communications such as these.

That's why there's a federal law in the U.S. that is intended to protect us from automated harassment. The Telephone Consumer Protection Act (TCPA) is a big bundle of contradictions. This statute allows for harsh financial penalties, but it is frequently ignored, violated, and disrespected. It is often dismissed as antiquated, yet it has expanded to cover new technologies. It has spawned hundreds of confusing court rulings, but many citizens have used it to sue corporations—and win—without hiring a lawyer. Sometimes it lets outrageous spamming activities slide through a loophole while punishing honest businesses that are trying to communicate with their customers. But despite all of that, it's essential. Repealing it would be a fatal blow to the delicate fabric that holds American society together.

Roughly 4,000 TCPA lawsuits are filed each year. Hundreds of millions of dollars change hands in these cases. The law has a significant effect on our lives, and on businesses of all sizes, but few people understand it very well. One of my goals with this book is to educate readers about the TCPA and the behind-the-scenes corporate efforts to stifle it. If you think the telephone situation couldn't get any worse than it is today, imagine if there were no restrictions whatsoever on unwanted telemarketing calls and texts. You might be surprised at how close we've come to that scenario.

Mostly, however, I'm hoping to enthrall you with a fascinating and thought-provoking tale. The history of robocalling is a back-and-forth epic battle between good and evil. There are heroes and villains, victories and defeats, and at least five or six of the deadly sins. There are heated First Amendment debates, sinister attempts to evade the law, and devastating courtroom verdicts. All of this is told with humor and with heaps of ridicule directed to those who deserve it—and to a few who don't. If this isn't the funniest book about telecommunications law that you've read this year, then I haven't done my job.

You're probably thinking that telemarketers are in for rough treatment in this book. On the hierarchy of least trusted professions, they fall somewhere between pharmaceutical company executives and North Korean dictators. But if you are a telemarketer who legally promotes a useful product, I offer you my sympathy since you are either unemployed or soon will be. That's because you are forbidden from contacting people who are on the Do-Not-Call list, which at this point includes almost every man, woman, and child in the U.S. The only one not on the list is 86-year-old Wilma Donkins of Havre, Montana. And that lady has a really bad temper and a foul mouth, so you better not try to sell her another *Reader's Digest* subscription that she already has.

As it turns out, telemarketers are just a small part of the robocalling industry. You will see this in the Prologue, which explains my personal story of how I became interested in this topic. Next, there is a discussion of the origins of the TCPA and its struggle to survive several court challenges. This is followed by a detailed description of the different categories of phone pests and how laws, court rulings, and technological changes have impacted each one. Then there is a look at the recent events that have made everything go crazy. Finally, in the Epilogue I briefly talk about using the law to claim the compensation that is rightfully yours. Don't expect a detailed "how-to" manual, but you'll have enough background information by that point that you shouldn't need one.

Although this is a work of non-fiction, there are no helpful footnotes containing case citations or other references.[1] Anything which might distract from the narrative has been shoved into a "Notes" section at the end. That's where you can check to see if I'm making stuff up, and can also get the information that you need to stay up-to-date in the future.

Let's get started before the phone rings and ruins our day.

---

[1] You just had to look, didn't you?

PROLOGUE: ATTACK OF THE TRASH CALLS

On one evening in the summer of 2006, my home telephone rang while I was eating supper. "May I speak to Darnell?" asked the woman who had interrupted my dining experience. I told her that she had the wrong number, and then I went back to my unhealthy bachelor food. My microwaved burrito was going to drift from its optimal temperature if I didn't consume it quickly.

A similar event occurred the next night, as another lady wanted to talk to Darnell. Again, I explained that she had misdialed. Calls like this continued to arrive every couple of days, and I learned that they were coming from a company called GC Services. When I asked what "services" it provided, I didn't get an answer. "That's a private matter between us and Darnell," one of its employees explained.

Its business with Darnell may have been private, but GC Services sure wanted me to know something about it. Why else would its agents dial my number over and over again and drop these little hints? I had fun with them for a while, answering the phone with various accents whenever the Caller ID showed they were on the line. They were greeted by a hillbilly one evening, an English governess the next, and then a barely passable impersonation of Ronald Reagan. But I was growing tired of being bothered whenever I had barbecue sauce on my hands and a mouth full of mashed potatoes that flew everywhere when I spoke. My phone was starting to smell like a greasy Arby's bag that had been left in a hot car for three weeks.

Finally I lost my composure and made an intemperate remark. I asked one of the employees if being stupid was a requirement for working there. "We're not going to call you again!" she shouted angrily. "We don't need our people to be insulted!"

They did phone me a few more times after that, but clearly their heart was no longer in it. They didn't even enjoy my imitation of Casey Kasem counting down the top forty places where Darnell might be hiding. ("Number 40. He's in the washing machine.

Number 39. He moved to New Zealand...") My relationship with GC Services, which at one time had been so full of promise and excitement, was now irretrievably broken.

This experience was my initiation into a seedy world that I hadn't known existed. Over the next year or two I began to get numerous calls from other mysterious sources, and these weren't quite as pleasant as the ones from GC Services. Very few were from live people; they were mostly unimaginative and repetitive prerecorded messages. How was I going to try out my new material on a robot? It was frustrating to spend weeks perfecting my Dr. Phil impression without ever getting a chance to use it. And I could insult the robots all I wanted, but they still wouldn't stop calling.

Many of the robocalls included a name that had been dubbed into the message, identifying a person that the company was supposedly trying to reach. Some of the callers still yearned to speak with Darnell, but most were looking for other individuals. Often they asked for one of the neighbors on my street, as if it was my job to relay messages to people who I barely knew and who certainly had phones of their own. Other names had apparently been made up entirely. One of the robocalls asked me to press "1" if I was "Gino," a name that is rare in the U.S. among those of us who do not own pizzerias. Another caller desperately needed to discuss a "personal business matter" with someone named "Cow Boy." Put on your spurs and giddy up, stranger, since you'll need your horse to track him down.

Some of the robots were haughty or threatening. "It is in your best interest to call us back today," one of them said, in a tone that suggested that I might be the victim of a car bombing the next morning if I didn't. Another of the computerized voices, representing the pretentiously named firm of Glass Mountain Capital, sounded so constipated that I wanted to reach through the line and give it a Fiber One bar.

Despite the vast quantities of telephone equipment and electricity that were being directed toward these campaigns, it wasn't exactly Fortune 500 enterprises that were financing them. Many of the companies that called me were so pathetic that they couldn't even afford a proper name. They had to go by initials such as "MRS" or "RPM." One of the few that sounded like a real corporation was Allied Interstate. When I first heard this name, I thought it had something to do with interstate highways. Perhaps its employees drove the length of I-40 each week, scooping up roadkill and processing it into fur coats, hats, and meat. That would be a valuable service. Instead, its sole contribution to the economy was an endless series of automated telephone calls that lacked any obvious purpose.

And that was what puzzled me the most about these calls: the lack of purpose. Even though they were phoning me multiple times per day, the companies were making a deliberate effort to avoid having a conversation. The robocall messages asked me to call them back immediately at their toll-free numbers, but whenever I did I was put into an interminable hold queue. Occasionally I would answer an incoming call on the first ring, ready to offer up the phone number and address of every Darnell I had ever met, and the other party would inexplicably hang up immediately before I could convey this information.

One enigmatic entity—identified by Caller ID only as "Waterloo, Iowa"—called every weekday while I was at work. I would see the missed calls on my phone, yet he or she never left a message on my machine and never called back in the evenings when I was home. It was like a burglar who doesn't take anything, but trims his beard hair into the kitchen sink to let you know that he was there.

Since the volume of robocalls was now far outpacing those of legitimate communications, I purchased a call blocking device that was able to screen out the worst offenders. But during one week I left the call blocker unplugged while I was away on vacation. When I returned, my answering machine was full of so many robotic messages that it had run out of space. Ten of the messages were identical prerecorded spiels from an outfit that called itself "American Agencies," imploring me to return the calls immediately. I did so, and spoke with one of its employees after spending several minutes on hold. He said that his company didn't have any business with me and he didn't know why it was calling. However, he also told me that it would continue robodialing my number a little longer just to be sure.

After this incident, I decided to investigate these so-called businesses in more detail. My call blocker's logs showed that some of them had called more than fifty times. I searched the Caller ID numbers on the internet and found hundreds of comments from other people facing this bewildering barrage of phone spam. The Better Business Bureau had many similar complaints. The callers all claimed to be debt collectors, yet they mostly just repeatedly dialed the wrong numbers. When they did reach the person they were seeking, there rarely seemed to be a real debt to collect. To paraphrase a few of the typical complaints:

"They say I owe money on a Sears card. But I don't shop at Sears, because it's not 1952."

"These morons are asking my twelve-year-old daughter to pay a hospital bill from Alaska. She's never been outside of Delaware."

"The account is from ten years ago. I already paid it off once and now they are telling me to pay again."

Not everyone had a negative experience. Occasionally, I would find complimentary reviews of the companies that had called me. However, there always seemed to be something suspicious about these comments:

"The friendly and thoughtful customer service representatives at XYZ Receivables put me on a payment plan that meets my budget. XYZ abides by all laws and adheres to the highest ethical standards. The people whining here are a bunch of deadbeats who want to get something for free."

If this was true, the deadbeats appeared to be having their way. Those who ignored the persistent demands for payment rarely, if ever, faced any consequences beyond additional unwanted calls. There was never a lawsuit summons, a wage garnishment, or a nasty notation on a credit report. Hardly anyone even reported getting a bill in the mail. I had received at least a hundred phone calls for Darnell, but only one letter addressed to him—and it wasn't from any of the organizations that had been calling. Evidently, these companies were one-trick ponies. Without the ability to annoy people incessantly with cheap robocalls, they would cease to exist.

Although these questionable debt collection calls accounted for most of the phone traffic at my home, my records showed a few other types of unsolicited contacts. There were occasional political robocalls and pollsters, and several people begging for charitable donations. I had ignored five calls from a fundraising organization for firefighters, thereby guaranteeing that my home would be allowed to burn completely to the ground if it were ever to catch fire. But amidst all the noise, it was striking how few of the callers were actual telemarketers. There might have been two or three sales calls surrounded by the hundreds of others. There were also a couple of robocalls from someone named "Rachel," and those would prove to be a harbinger of things to come.

Now that I had a better idea of who the culprits were, I was intrigued. Still annoyed, but intrigued. I remembered hearing about a law that allows individuals to recover damages from the selfish companies making these types of automated calls. I decided to research it to learn what could be done. The answer turned out to be a lot more complicated than I could have imagined.

1. ERNEST WRITES A LAW

Ernest "Fritz" Hollings was a great man and a national hero. He fought bravely in the Army during World War II, and then returned home to South Carolina where he began a career in law and public service. After some time in the state legislature and a term as governor, he found his true calling: the United States Senate.

For thirty-eight years, Hollings brightened the Capitol with his eloquence and common sense. His quick wit and folksy sayings were a breath of fresh air in the stuffy world of Washington bureaucracy. A debate against Fritz was usually a losing proposition, as one brash challenger learned when he foolishly demanded that the senator take a drug test. "I'll take a drug test if you'll take an IQ test," Hollings retorted. Chalk up another easy re-election victory for the silver-haired statesman from Charleston.

Even in retirement, the senator was still distinguished among his peers. While most politicians will proudly revel in whatever tribute is given to them, Hollings actually asked for his name to be removed from a courthouse building. He wanted it to be renamed to honor a judge who he felt was more deserving. Then in 2016, at the age of ninety-four, he became the oldest living current or former member of the Senate. The youngest is Mitch McConnell, who has successfully filibustered his own thirty-fifth birthday for more than forty years.

But anyone who experiences half a century in politics is bound to have a bad decade at some point. For Hollings, it was the 1980s. First, he was made to publicly apologize to a Senate colleague after making an offensive remark about the other man's Jewish faith. Then his 1984 bid for the presidency, which was always a long shot proposition at best, met a quick and quiet end with his sixth place finish in the New Hampshire Democratic primary election. Meanwhile, Hollings was getting nowhere with promoting the issues he cared about. No one but him was interested in reinstating the military draft, and his goal of balancing the federal budget was falling more and more out of reach all the time. If he didn't reinvent himself soon, Hollings was in danger of becoming completely irrelevant.

When a politician's career needs a little kick in the butt to get it moving again, one of the most helpful things he can do is participate in a media circus. This opportunity presented itself to Fritz Hollings in 1985. A group of congressional wives, led by Senator Al Gore's wife Tipper, had become outraged by the lyrics that they were hearing in popular music. They demanded that offensive musical recordings be labeled and restricted to prevent young people from accidentally purchasing them and destroying their fragile lives. After some spousal nagging in the Gore household, the matter came before the Senate Committee on Commerce, Science, and Transportation. Several well-known musicians were summoned to the Capitol to defend their songcraft, and plenty of television cameras would be there to cover the spectacle.

In advance of the hearing, the wives assembled a list of offensive rock songs that they dubbed "The Filthy Fifteen." Popular hits by Prince, Madonna, and Cyndi Lauper were suddenly exposed as the wicked odes to Satan that they were. When Madonna sang that she would like to dress her listeners up with her love, these world-wise women were not fooled by the song's seemingly innocent references to clothing. They knew exactly what the singer meant. "I'm a fairly with-it person, but this stuff is curling my hair," Tipper Gore said.

As the ranking Democratic member of the committee, Hollings was permitted to make one of the first opening statements. This was the aging senator's big chance to connect with a younger generation of voters. He could have used this moment to demonstrate both an appreciation of modern entertainment and a deep understanding of the First Amendment. Hollings could have defended the rights of recording artists—even that naughty temptress Cyndi Lauper—to express their artistic visions, just as he had defended his country's freedoms during the war. But he instead denounced the music as "porn rock" and "outrageous filth," and vowed to do everything within his power to combat it. "If I could find some way constitutionally to do away with it, I would," he said.

The rest of the hearing went no better for Hollings and his colleagues. The legendary singer-songwriter John Denver was called to testify, in the hopes that he might be the one and only popular performer who was unfashionable enough to support the committee's efforts. Several of the senators told him how much they enjoyed his music, but the flattery had no effect on Denver. He stated his firm opposition to censorship in any form, and criticized the record labeling plan that had been proposed by the senators' wives. Avant-garde musician Frank Zappa also spoke, and he compared the women's demands to "treating dandruff by decapitation."

The final music star to testify was Dee Snider, the lead singer of the hard rock band Twisted Sister. The band's hit song "We're Not Gonna Take It" had been listed as one of The Filthy Fifteen, a designation that annoyed Snider to no end. In reality, there was nothing at all offensive about the song's lyrics. It was the cartoonish violence of its music video that earned it a spot on the list. Tipper Gore had also accused Twisted Sister of producing a sexist T-shirt depicting "a woman in handcuffs sort of spread-eagled." Snider had never seen such a shirt, and considered this accusation to be slanderous. He arrived with a chip on his shoulder and was in no mood to kowtow to the committee. In his opening statement, he asserted that the federal government and the senators' wives had no authority to judge his music or to restrict it in any way.

Hollings decided to challenge Snider on this claim. Reverting to his training as a lawyer, he invoked the *Pacifica* case that he thought established the government's right to regulate indecent entertainment. This case has its origins in 1973, when a New York radio station broadcast an uncensored George Carlin comedy routine entitled "Filthy Words." Carlin's monologue listed the seven words that can never be uttered over radio or television, and provided numerous examples of their usage. The Federal Communications Commission (FCC) received a complaint from a man who had, for some unknown reason, decided to listen to the comedy routine on the radio while his young son was riding with him in the car. The Commission agreed with the complainant (and with the comedian) that these seven words were unfit for the public airwaves. It then issued the ultimate sanction: it placed a warning letter in the radio station's administrative file. (As we'll see again later, the penalties for violating a FCC rule are usually either inconsequential or draconian. They are rarely anywhere in between.)

The broadcaster wasn't willing to accept this bit of non-discipline and move on. It contested the FCC's authority to regulate the content of its programs. After the radio station won the initial round before a three-judge panel, the government appealed the matter to the U.S. Supreme Court. In 1978, the Court ruled by a slim 5-4 margin that the rules against "obscene, indecent, or profane language" on the radio were constitutional. They were *not* a violation of the free speech guarantees of the First Amendment.

Although the Supreme Court didn't want to hear this language on the radio, it had no problem with the same words appearing on paper. So, it attached a transcript of Carlin's routine to its opinion. Soon the Government Printing Office was churning out copies of the "Filthy Words" monologue—with "shit" repeated roughly seventy times—for distribution to libraries, schools, and law offices all over the country.

Hollings was convinced that the *Pacifica* ruling was relevant to the issue of record labeling. He confronted Snider with a quote from the Court's opinion: "Patently offensive, indecent material presented over the airwaves confronts the citizen not only in public, but also in the privacy of the home, where the individual's right to be left alone plainly outweighs the First Amendment rights of an intruder." But it was obvious, even from this small portion of the ruling, that *Pacifica* simply did not apply. It was clearly limited to radio and television broadcasts, not to the record store merchandise being discussed by the committee. The musician had to remind the senator of the distinction:

> "We're talking about the airwaves as opposed to a person going with their money to purchase an album to play in their room, their home, on their own time. The airwaves are something different. I think that the FCC and even MTV have done a fair job in keeping profanity, obscenity, and things like that off the public airwaves."

Hollings had no effective comeback to this. The distinguished statesman had somehow managed to lose a constitutional law debate to a jeans-clad, long-haired heavy metal rocker.

All things considered, it could have been worse. Al Gore had been smarmy and condescending while addressing the musicians; Hollings was merely ill-informed. However, when network news reported on the hearing, the most memorable sound bites came from the South Carolinian's opening statement. His over-the-top excoriations of the controversial songs, and his belligerent threats to outlaw them, were fodder for comedians. To complete the mockery, Frank Zappa included samples of the senators' voices in a music track entitled "Porn Wars." Hollings was featured prominently in this recording, with his cringe-worthy "outrageous filth" and "porn rock" lines repeated again and again for full effect.

The phrase "jumping the shark" had not yet been popularized in 1985, but for Hollings and his career this was a shark-jumping moment. After the record labeling hearing, he was no longer one of the cool senators like Ted Kennedy or Joe Biden. He wasn't even one of the quietly efficient ones like Nancy Kassebaum or Pete Wilson. Fritz Hollings was now, at age 63, officially an old grump. It didn't seem that he would ever again be a factor in an important national discussion.

But within a few years a new problem began bubbling to the surface of society. A wave of computer-generated telephone calls was disrupting the lives of Americans on a daily basis. To understand this phenomenon and why it was such a big deal, it's necessary to first take a brief look at the history of telemarketing.

The world's first telephone call was made on March 10, 1876 to a Boston man named Thomas Watson. The strange contraption that had been sitting on his desk suddenly began speaking to him in the voice of his boss, the inventor Alexander Graham Bell. Watson had to have been stunned by this unprecedented event. He was probably even more surprised a few days later when he received the world's first telephone bill.

There is no record of the very first telemarketing call, but it was likely later in the day on March 10th. As word got around town about his invention, Bell was certainly inundated with calls from patent attorneys offering to help him file a claim before Thomas Edison could steal his idea. Later, when affluent consumers began to purchase telephones at the start of the 20th century, local merchants sometimes used the new-fangled device to contact housewives and offer them items for sale. These calls were not always appreciated. In 1909, a Rochester, New York woman complained to the *Union and Advertiser* newspaper about the frequent disruptions at her household:

"My hands were busy moulding bread yesterday morning, when I heard the bell ring, and upon responding was told by a woman just gone into business in a Main street building, that she had a fine line of curtains, and other hangings, which she would like me to see. Shortly afterwards an employee of a firm making extracts, solicited my patronage in the same way, and though I told him I did not wish to be annoyed again, by being called to the telephone to hear of the extracts, the afternoon brought another call from the same firm. Last week a number of my friends and I heard over the telephone of a Shakespearian actor who was to fill a long engagement here, and we were asked by an attaché of the theater to please get our seats early, as there would undoubtedly be a rush for tickets. These are samples of a telephone annoyance that I would like to be freed from."

There was not much of a science behind telephone sales until the late 1960s. That's when public relations executive Murray Roman started the first specialized telemarketing firm, Campaign Communications Institute of America. After first conducting a successful sales campaign for Ford Motor, he turned most of his attention toward political fundraising. His company worked for both Republicans and Democrats; it was an equal opportunity nuisance. Anyone who had given a contribution to either party could expect to be contacted and begged for more money in the next election cycle.

Roman soon realized that telemarketing was like singing: anyone could do it, but few people were doing it well. So in the 1970s, he wrote two influential books explaining how to run a profitable telemarketing operation. He emphasized that careful planning was essential to cut through advertising clutter and make a memorable impression on consumers. Roman's employees never wasted their time phoning random housewives and ad-libbing a bunch of nonsense about "extracts" or "Shakespearian actors." They only contacted people who they believed might have a favorable response. The agents were given a script to follow, with portions placed on index cards that could be shuffled around based on the progression of each call. If one of the targets balked at donating $500, the agent could flip to a different card that would explain what could be accomplished for $250. Ultimately, the donor would be left believing that he got a good deal, even though he would have been far better off never answering the phone.

Three developments caused telemarketing to accelerate in the 1980s. First, the breakup of the AT&T monopoly led to more competitive pricing for long distance phone service. Second, technology improvements such as improved dialing equipment were making call centers more efficient. And finally, there was the invention of the robocall: a recorded advertising message that could be delivered to thousands of phone numbers without the need for human agents. These automated calls were used sparingly at first, but became commonplace near the end of the decade.

Robocalls turned the economics of telemarketing on its head. Since the cost of each call was negligible, there was no longer any reason to bother with buying an expensive contact list that could be used to target your message. A single automatic dialer could call all 10,000 phone numbers in an exchange in less than two weeks. The response rates were always well under 1%, but the ability to call so many people with such minimal effort made robocalls attractive to small businesses. It was time to throw those Murray Roman books in the trash, because a new era had arrived.

By 1991, millions of robocalls were being made to Americans each day. For most people, the automated calls were their first experience with "spam"—a term that would not be applied to bulk advertising until a few years later. The numbers were small compared to the robocall explosion that would come twenty years later, but the effect was worse in some ways because the internet was not yet in common use. The telephone was usually the only way to contact a friend, family member, or business without writing a letter and waiting days or weeks for a response. And an unwanted incoming call was not just an annoyance; it prevented the phone from being used until the caller disconnected. On one occasion, a woman in Amsterdam, New York was unable to summon an ambulance for her injured child due to a prerecorded telemarketing call that had tied up her phone line.

Robocall dialers were often programmed to call phone numbers sequentially. This was a problem for large companies, hospitals, and universities that owned blocks of hundreds of adjacent numbers. Medical paging services were hit especially hard by the nuisance. A doctor in Pennsylvania told the *New York Times* that he received one of the calls on his voice pager while standing at the bedside of a patient who had just died. He and the bereaved family members were treated to the sound of a cheery advertisement for a Hawaiian vacation. "Nothing to lose!" the caller declared as the family wept.

There were few good options available for dealing with this crisis. Caller ID and call blocking services were not widely available, and using an unlisted phone number was of no help at all. Many states attempted to outlaw or restrict the prerecorded calls, but these laws were useless against out-of-state perpetrators. Seriously disruptive incidents might merit a lawsuit on grounds such as "trespass to chattels" or "intrusion on seclusion." However, this was a bit of a reach. These types of claims originated from the ancient common law of England, in which a typical case involved one farmer's sheep wandering onto another farmer's pasture. No attorney wanted to be the one who had to analogize phone spamming to an ovine encroachment. He or she would need a fairly elaborate barrister's wig for that courtroom speech.

Meanwhile, another abuse of technology had appeared, as some businesses were now advertising by sending unsolicited fax messages. "Junk fax" was a particularly effective way for restaurants to tell workers in nearby offices about their daily lunch specials. A salesman would stop by his office fax machine to look for the signed purchase order he was expecting from a client, and he'd walk away with a craving for the liverwurst-and-anchovy sandwich at Podo's Deli. His company was then stuck paying for the ink and paper for someone else's promotion.

Fixing these problems required a certain type of person: an old grump. America needed the kind of guy who wanted to round up lazy youths and force them into the Army. It needed a man who would angrily smash a John Denver album upon hearing that the singer gets high from the Rocky Mountains. America needed Fritz Hollings.

Hollings' position on song lyrics had been vindicated somewhat since the debacle of 1985. Elitists had laughed at his warnings that the music industry was on the road to damnation, but now there were rap groups recording explicit songs like "Me So Horny" and "F--- tha Police." The robocall epidemic seemed like another slippery slope. If nothing was done, the problem would get worse and worse. The senator hadn't fought the Nazis only to see his countrymen subjugated by these annoying new-fangled machines.

Hollings proposed legislation, entitled the "Automated Telephone Consumer Protection Act," that would ban almost all of the robotic calls as well as junk fax advertising. His forceful Senate speech in support of the law is an oration of lasting beauty. It deserves to be remembered in the same way that we think of the Gettysburg Address or the soliloquy from *Hamlet*:

> "Computerized calls are the scourge of modern civilization. They wake us up in the morning; they interrupt our dinner at night; they force the sick and elderly out of bed; they hound us until we want to rip the telephone right out of the wall. ... It is telephone terrorism, and it has got to stop."

The House of Representatives was already looking at the same issue, but from a different angle. As with the record labeling hearing from several years earlier, congressional spouses helped spur the legislators into action. Massachusetts Representative Ed Markey's wife, a doctor, had complained to him about the automated advertising calls that were being made to her pager. Markey spoke with a colleague from New Jersey, Representative Marge Roukema, about the matter. Roukema's husband was a psychiatrist. Perhaps he could prescribe something that would help Markey's wife cope with the problem?

But Dr. Roukema's pager was being bombarded with robocalls too, and he knew that there wasn't a pill strong enough to take away the feelings of helplessness and rage that they induced. So Markey came up with a better idea: he would make the calls illegal. There would be plenty of chances to medicate everyone later if the law didn't work out.

Markey's bill was titled the "Telephone Advertising Consumer Rights Act." It offered weaker rules against robocalls than the Hollings bill did. Doctors with pagers would be protected from the automated calls; the average family with a landline phone, not so much. However, Markey's proposal also laid the foundation for a Do-Not-Call list that would prevent telemarketers—even those that used live agents rather than recordings—from calling households that signed up.

The American people were clamoring for action, but the legislation faced a hurdle. A powerful lobbying group, the Direct

Marketing Association (DMA), was looking out for the interests of telemarketers. It would be a challenge to pass either of these bills without its support.

Fortunately, the DMA was dominated by traditional Murray Roman-style marketers who saw the new autodialing machines as a threat to their business. They predicted—quite accurately—that the scattershot approach of the robocallers would eventually cause consumers to ignore other phone solicitations that had been more carefully targeted. Outlawing the automated calls would be just fine with them.

The DMA's bigger worry was Markey's Do-Not-Call list. However, this proposal relied on regulations that would be issued by the FCC, and nobody knew what those would be like. In the end, the lobbyists decided to let this vague part of the law go through. They could take their chances later in front of the Commission, or maybe even in court, where the public's low opinion of telemarketers would be less of a factor than it was in Congress.

The Hollings bill passed the Senate by a voice vote on November 7, 1991. The House approved the Markey bill on November 18. Now it was time for negotiators to resolve the differences and produce a single piece of legislation that could pass both chambers. This congressional compromise process worked much more efficiently than it does today. No one was called a liar or a racist, and not once did someone stomp his feet and threaten to shut the government down if he didn't get his way. Very quickly, the final bill was ready.

The new law would be titled the "Telephone Consumer Protection Act" or "TCPA." It looked a lot like the bill Hollings had written, with Markey's Do-Not-Call list tacked on, but one of the most important parts of the Senate bill didn't survive the negotiation process unscathed. Some House members fretted that Hollings' proposed ban on robocalls to homes would endanger innocent uses of the technology, like a business telling one of its customers that an order was ready to be picked up, or that an invoice was due to be paid. A congressman from Oklahoma wanted reassurance that power companies would still be able to robocall customers to warn them of impending outages. Hollings had included a couple of exemptions designed to cover these types of things, but there was still some doubt about how the law would be applied.

Texas Representative John W. Bryant had a more serious concern. There was a company in his district, MessagePhone, Inc., that had invented a clever way to contact people who aren't able to answer their phones. For example, suppose a woman is on her way home from a business trip. Before she boards the plane, she wants to call her husband and remind him to tape *The Golden Girls*. (Remember, this was 1991. People did things like that.) However, he's out fishing with a couple friends and she can't reach him. MessagePhone to the rescue! The woman records a message, and the service dials her house every fifteen minutes until her husband finally returns, picks up the ringing phone, and hears her plea. He thinks, "Oh good, she's just now getting on the flight in Newark. I still have a few hours." The wife walks in twenty minutes later to find her husband and his fishing buddies trying on all of her dresses and waxing each other's armpits. This awkward moment was brought to you by MessagePhone, the lame forerunner to voicemail.

An inflexible rule against prerecorded calls would put this innovative company out of business. So, Bryant and several of his colleagues successfully argued for the law to be watered down. Instead of banning almost all robocalls to homes, as Hollings had originally planned, the FCC would have some discretion to decide which ones were OK. MessagePhone would, presumably, be allowed to exist for another three or four weeks before becoming obsolete on its own.

Congress needed to wrap things up before Thanksgiving so that everyone could go home. And they succeeded—barely. On Tuesday of Thanksgiving week, the House passed the merged bill. The Senate approved it on Wednesday. The final version of the law included rules against many types of automated calls, a ban on junk fax, and the beginnings of the Do-Not-Call list. One giddy lawmaker inexplicably threw in a provision to encourage more AM radio stations to operate at night. This bill had something for everyone.

There was only one last obstacle: President George H.W. Bush needed to sign the legislation. This wasn't a sure bet, because Bush's desk was known as the spot where good ideas went to die. Representative Roukema still ruefully remembered how, in the previous year, he had shot down the family leave bill that she had urged him to approve. Much of her re-election campaign was then spent apologizing for the president. Would this be another political disaster?

Bush was unenthusiastic about the bill, to put it mildly. He considered himself to be primarily a foreign policy president. He was most comfortable when he was bombing the Middle East or barfing on another world leader. Why was Congress wasting his time with domestic legislation like this? Besides, if there was anything Bush hated more than broccoli, it was government restrictions on commerce. To him, the TCPA looked like just another economy-strangling, job-killing regulation that would move the nation one step closer to Marxism.

But the president knew that it wasn't worth fighting against a measure that had such widespread support in Congress and among the public. On December 20, 1991, Bush signed the TCPA into law as an early Christmas present—and late Hanukkah present—for America. He did so while simultaneously encouraging the FCC to limit the law's reach so that "legitimate business activities" would not be affected. This is how you get to be president, boys and girls: learn how to take both sides of an issue.

Although the spotlight was on the White House that day, the real hero was Ernest "Fritz" Hollings. His time in the Senate had finally paid off with a law that would have an impact for decades to come.

Senator Ernest F. Hollings (1922-2019)
(U.S. Senate Historical Office)

2. THE TCPA: TRESPASSING CALLERS PUNISHED APPROPRIATELY

There was now finally some relief from those annoying automated calls that had plagued the nation. But not all categories of robocalls were treated equally under the TCPA, and not all types of phone lines were given the same level of protection from them.

The most urgent priority was to protect the healthcare system. It was now illegal to make an automated call to any emergency line, hospital patient room, or pager. There were two—and *only* two—exceptions. Calls made for an emergency purpose were exempt, and so were those made with the consent of the called party.

The same rules applied to mobile phones. Much like paging services, cellular networks used radio signals that had limited bandwidth. A large volume of automated calls would render the systems unavailable for other uses. Also, there was no such thing as unlimited minutes in 1991. If you were one of the lucky few to have a cell phone, you had to pay for every incoming and outgoing call. There were already a few anecdotal reports of robodialers calling cellular numbers with advertising messages, leaving the recipients stuck with the bill. The TCPA sought to nip this problem in the bud.

Two types of automated calls are included in this ban. The first is what most people think of as a robocall: a call that plays a prerecorded message or uses an artificial computer-generated voice. However, Congress realized that this wasn't sufficient. Someone could employ phone equipment in other mischievous ways that would tie up emergency lines or waste other people's money. So, the TCPA also made it illegal to call cell phones, pagers, and emergency numbers with automated dialing systems. If an autodialer is used, then it doesn't matter what the recipient hears when—or if—the call is answered. Maybe it will be a live performance of a newly discovered Mozart concerto by the London Symphony Orchestra, or maybe it will be a prerecorded ad for a tanning salon. Either way, the mere act of autodialing without permission is illegal.

"Automated dialing system" later became one of the most divisive three-word phrases in the United States, along with "build the wall" and "New England Patriots." There will be more to say about this in later chapters. But in 1991, there was virtually no objection to any of these rules about calls to pagers and cell phones. The exemptions for emergency calls and consensual calls seemed to be enough to cover any scenario in which someone might legitimately need to use an autodialer.

One marketing research company was not happy with this part of the law, however. This company's mission was to keep track of the number of cell phone subscribers in each city. Using software called "Celshare," it routinely dialed all phone numbers that were assigned to cellular carriers. Celshare would then tally up how many of these numbers were actually in use.

The company claimed that it tried to prevent anyone from being charged for these calls. How did it accomplish this? The Celshare system would call only in the middle of the night, and it would let the phone ring only once or twice before hanging up. By the time that the phone's panicked owner could jump out of bed, turn on a light, and dig her phone out of her purse, the call would usually be disconnected. So, the calls themselves may have been free to most of the recipients, but those extra espressos the next morning were beginning to add up.

This company petitioned the FCC for a special dispensation to let it continue interrupting everyone's sleep. The commissioners were incredulous at this request. For one thing, the new law was quite clear: using an autodialer in this way was absolutely forbidden. Congress hadn't given the FCC any authority to make an exception. Besides, this was exactly the kind of selfish and obnoxious behavior that *should* be illegal, and the TCPA was already proving its worth by putting an end to it. So it was time to say goodnight to Celshare. See you in hell, the Commission said, albeit not quite in those words.

But only about one out of every twenty Americans owned a mobile phone in the early 1990s. For most people, the bigger concern was the robocalls that were being made to their home landline phones. The TCPA banned these calls, but did so in a way that was much weaker than the rules for cell phones. Partly, this is because the restriction applies only to calls made with an artificial or prerecorded voice. There is no rule against using an automated dialing system, so if the Celshare people want to start calling landlines at 3 AM there would be nothing stopping them. The bigger weakness, however, is that this part of the law authorized the FCC to make exemptions to it. This was the compromise provision that the House had added to Hollings' original version of the bill. It was going to misfire in a way that few people predicted.

The FCC is an influential agency, but it does its best work when asked to decide purely technical matters. Suppose that you own a classic rock radio station in Michigan, and you want to install a directional antenna so that your signal can reach the lucrative Kalamazoo market. You must first apply to the Commission for a permit. Government engineers will then look at a map, pull out a slide rule, and figure out whether this change will cause interference with the gospel station in Lansing that transmits on the same frequency. Although this process involves some paperwork and expense for your radio station, it's much better than convincing Congress to pass a new law to authorize the antenna. Imagine hiring a team of lobbyists and making thousands of dollars in campaign contributions, only to have the president veto the Kalamazoo Radio Revitalization Act of 2020 because you didn't play his Doobie Brothers request when he was in town.

The outcome is usually muddled when the FCC involves itself in more substantive concerns. One of its first big challenges, back in the 1920s when it was still called the "Federal Radio Commission," was presented by charlatan physician John R. Brinkley. Brinkley used his AM radio station to promote an impotence cure that consisted of surgically implanting goat testicles into men. Although he boasted that a couple of goat glands could turn a lamb into a ram, the Commission believed that statements like this were not in the public's best interest. Nor were they any good for goats. The Commission revoked Brinkley's broadcasting license, leading to a lengthy fight in which the doctor avoided the censure for several years by transmitting from across the Mexican border. Although the government ultimately won this battle, it lost the war. Whenever AM radio airs an ad for a quack "male enhancement" product, which is approximately every eleven seconds, you can hear Dr. Brinkley laughing from the grave.

The FCC's attempts to regulate indecent programming have also been far from perfect. The Commission didn't even know which words were vulgar until George Carlin helpfully listed them. And, more recently, the network neutrality debate has turned into a showcase of everything that can go wrong when the FCC is forced to weigh in on an important issue.

When Congress banned robocalls to home phones, it asked the FCC to make exemptions for categories of calls that were determined not to be a nuisance or an invasion of privacy. Only calls that were made for non-commercial purposes, or that didn't include unsolicited advertisements, were eligible for possible exemptions. The Commission was also instructed to consider the free speech protections of the First Amendment as part of this equation. In other words, it had to do the work that the members of Congress didn't finish because they were in such a rush to leave town before Thanksgiving. This was a lot to demand of an agency that preferred to tinker with math and science stuff, like calculating how many megahertz are in a kilowatt. Congress would have had more success ordering the National Park Service to plan and execute an amphibious military invasion of Chile.

There was certainly a rationale for letting the Commission make a few exceptions to the ban. A service like MessagePhone was technically a robocall, since it played back a prerecorded voice, but it had nothing else in common with the spam calls that Congress was trying to restrict. It deserved to be spared. Additionally, President Bush had called for the FCC to exempt other "legitimate business practices." He specifically asked it to protect the automated calls that notify customers when a catalog order is available for pickup at a local store. Bush probably had a big shipment of garish patterned socks on the way from J.C. Penney and wanted to be sure that he didn't miss it.

However, there is no evidence that the FCC gave serious thought to the definitions of "nuisance," "invasion of privacy," or "legitimate business practices." It didn't ruminate for longer than three seconds on the proper balance between regulation and freedom of speech. On October 16, 1992, the Commission released its initial set of rules for enforcing the TCPA. These rules declared that the *only* robocalls to homes that would be banned were those containing unsolicited commercial advertisements for products or services. All others would be exempted. Under the terms outlined by Congress, this was the biggest possible loophole that the FCC was allowed to create.

This dubious decision set the stage for two of the biggest problems with the TCPA. First, it vindicated activities that were clearly a nuisance by any measure. Among debt collectors and non-profit fundraisers, in particular, it kicked off a race to the bottom to see who could abuse telephone technology the most. Second, it caused many organizations—some legitimate, others less so—to build their outreach practices around this loophole. As homeowners began ditching their landlines and replacing them with mobile phones, these entities were often surprised to learn that a lot of their calls were no longer legal. They then needed to spend millions of dollars to hurriedly upgrade their procedures. In some cases, they didn't find out until it was too late.

And so, for better or worse, the restrictions on automated calls to cell phones and home phones were in place. That left one other major category: business phones. As part of the new law, Congress instructed the FCC to consider implementing rules that would protect businesses against abusive robocalling practices. But, like a teenager who pretends not to hear his parents telling him to mow the lawn, the Commission almost completely ignored this request. They mentioned it only in a footnote, saying they were "not persuaded" that any such rules were necessary. Commercial phone customers would have to be content with a rarely enforced provision that bars autodialers from tying up two phone lines of a business at the same time.

For businesses, the greater benefit of the TCPA was its ban on junk faxes. These were defined as unsolicited commercial advertisements; most charitable and political messages were, once again, exempt. Rounding out the rest of the statute, there were some new technical requirements that applied to both robocalls and faxes. And finally, there was Markey's Do-Not-Call list proposal, which accomplished very little at the time because all of the action was delegated to the FCC. We'll revisit the Do-Not-Call list later when something interesting actually happens. (Hint: It isn't until 2003.)

All of this can be a little confusing, but maybe a picture will help. This Venn diagram shows what types of calls are restricted by the TCPA, based on the type of phone that is called:

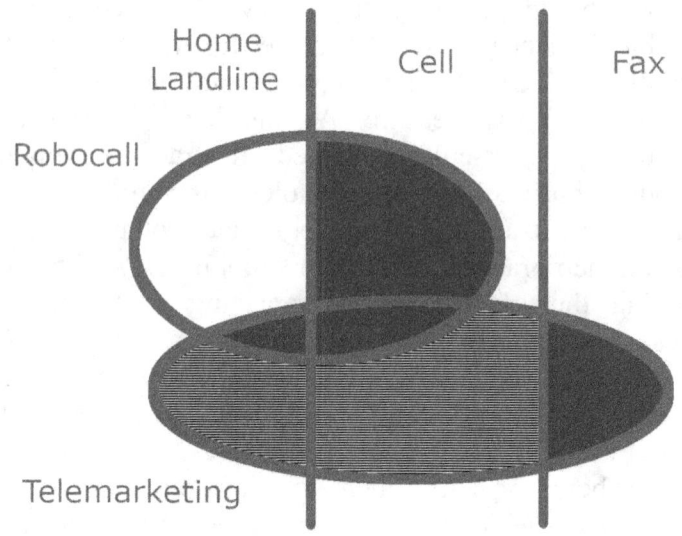

The fully darkened parts of each ellipse are calls that are generally prohibited without prior consent. The lighter gray areas are subject to potential Do-Not-Call rules. The white part of the "Robocall" ellipse is the FCC's loophole.

Unfortunately, there are other types of nuisance calls that aren't contemplated here. When your girlfriend rings you up at work to give you a twenty-five minute plot summary of a Hallmark TV movie that she watched, it's annoying but legal. When Bart Simpson dials Moe's Tavern and asks to speak to Al Coholic or Ivana Tinkle, that's also an unwanted call that isn't covered by the TCPA. We will have to wait for another heroic senator, a Fritz Hollings of the future, to write a law that protects people from those infuriating situations.

So, the TCPA certainly had some limitations, but the real measure of a law is how well it can be enforced. We're all familiar with rules that no one ever obeys, since there are simply no consequences for breaking them. For example, many restaurants have a placard in the bathroom that says "Employees Must Wash Hands." Sometimes there's an official-sounding citation at the bottom of the sign, such as "City of Pascagoula, Public Health Code No. 13-5." However, you can stand in there for an hour as employees go in and out, and not one of them will wash your hands—even if you point to the sign and ask politely. They learned on their first day of the job that the sign was nothing more than a paper tiger. Eventually, most customers just wipe their hands on their pants and hope for the best.

At the federal level, the task of enforcing the TCPA should have been given to the FBI, the Secret Service, or perhaps the Navy SEALs. Instead, the FCC—the same agency that tunneled a gaping hole through the law in 1992—is in charge of pursuing violators. And even if the Commission actually wants to enforce the statute, it has one hand tied behind its bureaucratic back. It is empowered to fine robocallers and junk faxers up to $10,000 for each illegal call, but first it has to issue a warning citation to the offender. Only those who don't heed the warnings can be punished.

Enforcement at the state level is not much better. If a state attorney general receives complaints about a TCPA violator, he is permitted to file a lawsuit on behalf of the victims. In practice, however, most state governments are not interested in doing the FCC's job. A few states have laws that are more thorough than the federal legislation, and it makes more sense to enforce those instead. For example, Indiana—not normally a hotbed of progressive legislation—has banned most prerecorded calls since 1988. While the rest of the nation contended with the FCC exemption that unleashed billions of unwanted robocalls to landline phones, Hoosiers were enjoying relative peace.

But the TCPA also contains an unusual and extraordinary feature that is the envy of other laws: a "private right of action." If you receive an unlawful robocall or junk fax, you don't have to just sit around waiting for the FCC or your state attorney general to do something about it. You may sue the violator on your own for $500. If the court finds that a caller willfully or knowingly violated the statute, the amount may be increased to a maximum of $1,500. You can also obtain an injunction: an order from the court that bars the perpetrator from illegally calling you again, under penalty of a contempt charge and possible jail time.

While there are other laws that have a private right of action, the TCPA is special in a couple of respects. First, it is stackable. In other words, the penalties for separate violations are added together with no upper limit on how high they can go. For example, if someone is boorish enough to illegally robocall you fifty times, then he (it's rarely a "she") must pay you a *minimum* of $25,000. It does no good for him to grovel before the judge with a sad story about why he should be let off easy. Maybe his robocalling habit can be blamed on a maladjusted childhood, low SAT scores that kept him out of community college, and years of inhalant abuse that have putrefied his brain. It's all probably true, but it doesn't matter. The court has no discretion to lower the amount, and might even triple it if the perpetrator grovels a little too much. As the late Johnnie Cochran might have said: "You do the ring, you buy the bling."

The other thing that makes this law very powerful is strict liability. The usual standard for winning a lawsuit is negligence: the defendant failed to take reasonable precautions and caused a foreseeable harm to someone else. Strict liability is typically reserved for cases involving defective products or inherently dangerous activities such as the use of explosives. It means that a plaintiff can win compensation without having to prove that there was any carelessness or malicious intent. With strict liability, the TCPA puts autodialers in the same category as dynamite. You had better not use them unless you know *exactly* what you are doing.

Here's an example of the pitfalls of robocalling. Suppose that "Madame Mystical, the Telephone Psychic" offers a free service that sends subscribers an automated call every morning with her predictions for the day. And suppose that one of her subscribers changes phone numbers without notifying her. Some other person then begins getting these automated calls on his new cell phone, without having given consent for them. If the new recipient is particularly clever, he will not do anything to try to stop the daily nuisance. He will put up with it for nearly four years—which is the statute of limitations for the private right of action—and then sue Madame Mystical for $730,000. That probably wasn't one of her predictions.

Of course, most robocallers aren't quite so innocent as in this contrived example. And it is the private right of action, far more than any threat from federal or state authorities, that keeps them on edge. Imagine being able to turn the tables on someone who has engaged in repulsive behavior—and walk away with a nice profit. That's the beauty of the TCPA.

3. THE COURTS HAVE THEIR SAY

The First Amendment says that "Congress shall make no law ... abridging the freedom of speech." Since the TCPA abridges some forms of speech, and it was made by Congress, it was certain to attract a challenge to its constitutionality. It didn't help that its lead author was Senator Hollings, a man who had once lost a First Amendment debate to the dude from Twisted Sister. Maybe if telemarketers enlisted the aid of an even greater legal mind—perhaps Ozzy Osbourne or Eddie Van Halen—they could persuade a court to overturn the new law.

But Hollings had learned a lesson from the rock music fiasco. From the outset, he prepared a counterattack to any criticism of the TCPA. In a Senate committee report, he cited his favorite line from the *Pacifica* ruling again: "in the privacy of the home ... the individual's right to be left alone plainly outweighs the First Amendment rights of an intruder." This time the quote was far more appropriate than it had been when the senator used it in the record labeling hearing. It was a major stretch to call a Madonna album an "intruder" when a purchaser had willingly brought it home from a store. If anything, the suggestive record was more like an inebriated guest who overstays his welcome after a party. But an unsolicited robocall was a telephonic trespass and an affront to the quietude of a dwelling. It clearly met the definition of an intruder.

Hollings had strived to make the TCPA content-neutral, meaning that it would be applied equally to all types of prerecorded calls. Commercial sales calls would be treated the same as political robocalls, informational calls, and fundraising calls. A content-neutral law is difficult to challenge on First Amendment grounds. As long as an important government interest is at stake, and the law allows other methods of sending the same message, it is likely to be upheld by the courts.

Unfortunately, the senator's original vision for the law was compromised during the negotiations with the House of Representatives. The rule against autodialed and prerecorded calls to cell phones, pagers, and emergency lines was still content-neutral.

That part of the statute was unassailable. However, robocalls to home phones were now subject to an FCC exemption that discriminated against companies offering goods or services for sale. This was a content-based restriction. The burden was on the government to prove that it was constitutional, and it would be an uphill fight.

The federal courts were accustomed to reviewing, and often rejecting, similar attempts to regulate commercial speech. One of the most influential cases of this kind was decided in 1980. The Central Hudson Gas & Electric Corporation wanted to run advertisements encouraging people to consume more electricity. Its most profitable customers were those who left their refrigerator doors hanging open half the day, or who used their electric hair dryers to slowly torture spiders to death. However, the New York utility commission refused to allow marketing messages that conflicted with its goal of conserving energy. Central Hudson challenged the rule as a violation of its First Amendment rights.

Although the utility commission's intentions were good, the Supreme Court ruled that it had overreached. Its ban was so broad that Central Hudson couldn't even run ads telling people to shift their energy usage to off-peak times, or to switch from gas heating to electric. Simply put, the commission's marketing policy wasn't a "reasonable fit" to its stated objective.

Kathryn Moser was the owner of a chimney sweeping business in the Salem, Oregon area. She wasn't an expert on First Amendment law, and had probably never heard of the *Central Hudson* case. However, she knew firsthand the benefits of automated advertising calls. Her company had been unprofitable until she purchased a robocalling machine and began notifying local residents that chimney sweeps were still a thing. (Most people had assumed they existed only in Dickens novels and *Mary Poppins*.) Soon, dozens of curious homeowners were engaging Moser's services in the hopes of seeing small children scurrying up their fireplaces to remove hazardous deposits of soot and creosote.

But with the passage of the TCPA, Moser's $1,800 machine would soon be useless. Meanwhile, larger businesses that could afford to make telemarketing calls with live operators were permitted to continue their practices. Also, thanks to the FCC's loophole, non-profit groups were still allowed to solicit donations with prerecorded calls. That didn't seem fair to her.

Moser joined together with Ray Kolker, whose company had sold her the robodialer, and formed a trade group: the National Association of Telecomputer Operators. She then challenged the TCPA's constitutionality in federal court. Judge James Redden agreed with her that the law was not content-neutral because of the exemption for non-commercial calls. So, the rule from *Central Hudson* would apply. The law would be upheld only if it was a "reasonable fit" to the government's goal of protecting people from unwanted telephone intrusions into their home. And the judge concluded that the distinction between commercial and non-commercial calls was, in fact, unreasonable:

> "Both kinds of telemarketing calls trigger the same ring of the telephone; both kinds of calls invade the home equally, and both risk interrupting the recipient's privacy equally. Under the TCPA, noncommercial entities may use machines to deliver prerecorded messages, which further moots the attempted distinction: both kinds of calls deprive the recipient of human interplay, both risk delivering a message to an inappropriate party, and both risk fouling the means by which telephone subscribers can record callers' messages."

Then Redden took it a step further. He stated that the distinction between prerecorded advertising and live telemarketing was also unreasonable, because consumers found both types of calls almost equally annoying. Furthermore, Kolker had somehow convinced the judge that only about 3% of telemarketing calls were prerecorded. (The FCC's statistics showed that the actual percentage was far higher.) A law that reduced the volume of unwanted calls by such a tiny fraction could hardly be called a "reasonable fit" to the problem.

So, because of a chimney sweep in Oregon, the most important part of the TCPA was barred from going into effect. It appeared that the law's future was as dark as two-week-old guacamole. The government appealed the ruling, however, and the judges of the 9th Circuit Court of Appeals had a completely different point of view than Judge Redden. They focused only on the words of the statute, not on the FCC's discriminatory exemption for non-commercial calls. By this measure, the TCPA was content-neutral and the "reasonable fit" rule from *Central Hudson* was irrelevant. The court's task was to instead determine whether the law was a valid "time, place, and manner restriction" on a mechanism of speech.

There are many examples of time, place, and manner restrictions that have been upheld by the courts. For example, some communities have a zoning rule that bars adult entertainment businesses and churches from being located within a thousand feet from each other. Clearly, both of these types of establishments have First Amendment rights that are worthy of protection. It would also be convenient for them to be on the same block, since you could walk to a strip club after Sunday morning Mass without even getting back in your car. However, houses of worship can sometimes bring up repressed feelings of guilt. Imagine strolling out of a video store with a brand new copy of *Darnell Does Des Moines*, only to see Jesus scowling angrily at you from a crucifix on the roof of a nearby church. The government has a compelling interest in protecting adult businesses and their patrons from such unnecessary shame, and so zoning regulations such as these have been found to be constitutional. You're still free to open up a new church, but you have to put it where it won't interfere with someone else's happiness.

The appeals court ruled that the TCPA was an appropriate time, place, and manner restriction that was narrowly tailored by Congress to address a specific problem. Even if it only reduced annoying calls by 3%, it was better than nothing. Also, it didn't completely stop Moser's company from using the telephone to advertise its services to the community. Moser could continue to use prerecorded messages, as long as she introduced the messages with a live solicitor who obtained consent to play a recording. "That some companies prefer the cost and efficiency of automated telemarketing does not prevent Congress from restricting the practice," the court said.

The TCPA had been slated to go into effect on December 20, 1992, exactly one year after its signing. The appellate court's opinion, upholding the constitutionality of the robocall restriction, was issued on February 9, 1995. Moser's challenge had bought businesses an additional two years in which they could continue making the advertising robocalls that people hated, but now the reckoning had come. When the Supreme Court refused to hear her appeal of the 9th Circuit's ruling, the National Association of Telecomputer Operators was forced to disband. As a final insult, the word "telecomputer" was purged from the English language, never to be spoken in polite company again.

The junk fax portion of the law was challenged separately by five small businesses that used this controversial marketing technique. They hired the same law firm that represented Moser and her group, and once again the dispute went before a federal judge in Oregon. At first glance, the government's chances of defending this part of the statute did not look very good. The TCPA bans only unsolicited faxes that advertise "the commercial availability or quality of any property, goods, or services." This is a classic example of a content-based restriction, and this time there was no way to blame the FCC. Congress had written the discriminatory language directly into the law.

The businesses argued that the junk fax restriction was unfair because it didn't also apply to non-profit fundraising or political faxes. It didn't even outlaw prank faxes that were specifically intended to waste paper and ink. However, the court decided that the TCPA was a reasonable solution to the problem of advertising costs being shifted onto unwilling recipients. Simply put, the law passed the *Central Hudson* test. The companies appealed the ruling to the 9th Circuit, but to no avail. The junk fax ban was upheld.

There was one last serious effort to overturn this part of the law, but it didn't come until several years later. In 1999 and 2000, the state of Missouri tracked down two companies that it believed were responsible for a deluge of unwanted fax ads that were plaguing businesses in the state. The logical thing for the perpetrators to do would have been to deny everything. When the investigators knocked on the front door, they could have distracted them for a few minutes while the fax machines and other pieces of evidence were smuggled out the back door and tossed into the nearest creek. But that wasn't an option in this case, because these two defendants—Fax.com and American Blast Fax—had been openly bragging about their ability to send large volumes of spam faxes. Oops. So it was time for plan B, which was to admit that they had violated the TCPA, but then argue that the law was unconstitutional and couldn't be enforced.

The case was heard by Judge Stephen Limbaugh, a Ronald Reagan appointee who was part of a celebrated family of conservative Missouri lawyers, judges, and commentators. You may have heard of his nephew Rush, who is the most trusted AM radio personality of modern times. (If Rush Limbaugh tells you to implant goat organs into your body—and he probably will at some point—you better do it.) The judge knew that the liberal 9th Circuit had upheld the TCPA, but his court was part of the 8th Circuit. He was free to make up a different rule, and he did.

Judge Limbaugh was skeptical that junk faxes were even a problem. When Congress decided to ban them, it didn't do any empirical studies or solicit any expert testimony on the economic loss caused by each fax. The cost to the recipient could be an insignificant two cents, or it could be forty cents or more. No one had a definite answer. Besides, the law was passed in 1991, and the cost had certainly dropped since then. Fax machines no longer required expensive specialized paper, and many faxes were being automatically converted into emails instead of being printed at all. Since the government had not demonstrated a substantial interest in preventing junk fax, Limbaugh concluded that the law was a violation of the First Amendment. There was no need for him to consider the "reasonable fit" part of the *Central Hudson* test, though he did anyway and deemed the TCPA a failure by that measure as well.

For those wishing that the TCPA would go away, this was the last hurrah. The Missouri attorney general and the FCC appealed the judge's ruling to the 8th Circuit. The appellate court contradicted Limbaugh, saying that the government was free to rely on anecdotal evidence or even on "common sense" in determining that junk faxes were a costly nuisance. (Whether Congress is capable of possessing common sense is another matter.) Furthermore, the latest evidence indicated that technological advancements had barely made a dent in the problem. Eighty percent of faxes were still being printed on paper, and unwanted advertisements were costing many small businesses $100 a year or more just for wasted supplies.

Limbaugh was overruled for these reasons, and the law was upheld. Both Fax.com and American Blast Fax were forced out of business. Fax.com's valuable internet domain name was then acquired and repurposed by one of the companies that had sued it for violating the TCPA. This is the corporate equivalent of doing a tap dance on an adversary's grave, only far more profitable.

Incidentally, Judge Limbaugh was not always the champion of free speech that this case might make you believe. When St. Louis County, Missouri passed an ordinance restricting the sale of violent video games, the judge heard a First Amendment challenge to the law from a trade association. In his decision, Limbaugh likened video games to other competitive pastimes such as baseball, bingo, and boxing. He concluded that a mere game or sport was devoid of expressive conduct, and so it was not entitled to any protection under the law. (This was probably a shock to Major League Baseball, which had long been using the copyright laws to prevent fans from disclosing the descriptions or accounts of games without express written permission.) Not surprisingly, the 8th Circuit overruled the judge once again.

By the time the junk fax cases were completely settled, it was 2003. That was the same year that Fritz Hollings announced he would soon retire from the U.S. Senate. He could do so with satisfaction, knowing that he had written a popular law that was resilient to constitutional challenge. However, some parts of the TCPA were prone to differences of interpretation. In this respect, Hollings could have learned something from his old nemesis, Twisted Sister. When Dee Snider belted out the lyrics of "We're Not Gonna Take It," there was no question about what he meant. Sure, the word "it" is vague by itself, but the ambiguity was resolved by the band's music videos that were played non-stop on MTV in the 1980s. In these videos, parents and teachers who placed unreasonable demands on teen metal-heads were ejected out of second-story windows and into swimming pools by the raw force of rock 'n' roll. Plainly, the members of Twisted Sister were unwilling to accept *any* authoritarian nonsense—without exclusion or limitation. If Congress had only made a video to go along with the TCPA, it would have saved a lot of confusion later.

The confusion extended to a very basic matter: no one was entirely certain which courts were allowed to hear TCPA lawsuits. When Senator Hollings was writing the law, he envisioned that most of the cases would be decided in small claims courts. The rules here are more relaxed than they are in the "grown up" courts. As a small claims plaintiff or defendant, you don't have to learn complicated rules of evidence. You don't have to sit for a day-long deposition. You might not even need to change out of your pajamas before coming to your hearing. What's not to like?

The best thing about filing a small claims suit is that your dispute may be picked for arbitration on *Judge Judy*. Many of the cases on this TV show involve acquaintances who have had a falling out. Often they are former roommates fighting over the communal Nintendo system or last month's utility bills. The judge reviews the facts of each case prior to each show, and sometimes seems to have made up her mind before even hearing any testimony. She snarls and snaps at one of the parties as if they have just peed on her leg and told her it was raining. It is great entertainment.

It's fun to imagine how Judge Judy would handle a TCPA case:

> Judge Judy: "So, Mr. Lumpeldorff, you own a collection agency that robocalled the plaintiff's cell phone. Is that correct?"
>
> Defendant: "Yes, your honor, but—"
>
> Judge Judy: "But-but-but. I don't want to hear 'but.' You broke the law and now your firm has to pay damages. What's the name of your company?"
>
> Defendant: "It's called XYZ Receivables."
>
> Judge Judy: "XYZ Receivables! You're the same fools who left me thirty spam voicemails for 'Judy Judge' and 'Judge Reinhold.' Byrd, lock him up!"
>
> Bailiff Byrd: "Judge, we don't have a jail in the studio. I think the walls here are made of cardboard."
>
> Defendant: "Those messages weren't spam, your honor. They were timely payment reminders."
>
> Judge Judy: "Timely payment reminders?! Are you kidding me? Don't pee on my phone and tell me it fell in the toilet!"

The TCPA allows a private right of action to be brought in an "appropriate" state court "if otherwise permitted by the laws or rules of court of a State [or of a syndicated TV judge]." The first such cases were, in fact, filed in the small claims courts administered by the states and their individual counties and cities. The typical defendant was a local business, maybe a handyman service or a fitness club, that had run an illegal robocalling or fax marketing campaign. Plaintiffs were picking up anywhere from $500 to around $5,000 each time, and were able to keep almost all of it since they rarely needed to hire a lawyer. A few of the plaintiffs wrote books or web pages to share their wisdom so that others could learn how to sue telemarketers for fun and profit. Most of the time, the law was working just as Hollings had hoped.

However, there were some drawbacks. Federal laws are usually enforced in federal courts, so the TCPA's reference to state court venues was highly unusual. State judges, especially those at the lowest levels, often didn't know anything about this law. They had to be educated first, and then they had to be convinced that they were permitted to hear the cases. In Texas, the state supreme court simply refused to allow any TCPA actions to be filed in the state until the legislature eventually passed a law telling them to do so.

Jurisdictional problems in the local courts sometimes made it hard to bring out-of-state defendants to justice. The town magistrate in White Owl, South Dakota was unlikely to issue a subpoena for a major national company's phone records, or force its chief technology officer to fly in from New York to testify about its dialing system. Also, the differences in state court systems led to variability in the enforcement of the law. For example, most states wouldn't let plaintiffs sue for violations occurring more than a year or two in the past, even though federal laws like the TCPA normally had a four-year statute of limitations.

Meanwhile, the amount of money at stake began to grow. As the adoption of cell phones increased, more types of organizations were finding themselves in the crosshairs of the law. Some businesses had ineptly robocalled the same wireless phone numbers repeatedly, hundreds of times, and had attracted lawsuits asking for damages of over $100,000. The bigger development, though, was the advent of the TCPA class action. There was nothing stopping attorneys from filing multi-million dollar suits on behalf of thousands—or, in some instances, millions—of people who were victimized by a single company's illicit telephone practices. Nothing, that is, except the restrictions and general stubbornness of the state courts, some of which made class actions virtually impossible. It was becoming clear that many TCPA cases would be handled more fairly and consistently if they were tried in the federal court system.

Here's where Congress' lack of clarity was a problem. The law said that state courts could hear TCPA cases, if they felt like it, but it was silent about the role of the federal courts. In the 6th and 7th Circuits, which included much of the Great Lakes region, federal courts were accepting the cases nonetheless. They ruled that the claims involved a question of U.S. law, and so they were able to exercise jurisdiction. However, at least six of the other circuits decided to reject private TCPA claims, saying that they must be filed in state courts as Congress had decreed. It was a classic circuit split, a disagreement at the highest levels of the judiciary. Only the justices of the U.S. Supreme Court could say who was correct, but first someone needed to ask them their opinion. They don't just sit around and rule on things for the hell of it.

The hero of the story is a Florida man named Marcus Mims. In 2008, he received a series of unwanted prerecorded messages on his cell phone. They were from an Illinois company, Arrow Financial Services, that was trying to contact him about an allegedly overdue student loan. It might be interesting to know more details about this. Was Mims really having trouble paying his loan, or was Arrow barking up the wrong tree? Did his debt originate from one of those for-profit schools that charges fifty grand for a worthless, overly specialized degree in a major like Alpaca Shearing Technology or Church Pew Maintenance? But his financial misfortune was not the real issue. Arrow didn't have his permission to make the robocalls, and now it would be the one owing a debt to him.

Mims believed that Arrow had violated the TCPA as well as federal and state laws about debt collection. For tactical reasons, it was better for him to sue in federal district court than to take his chances in the chaotic local courts of southern Florida. However, his state was part of the 11th Circuit, which had previously ordered the dismissal of all private TCPA claims from federal court. He sued anyway, urging the judges to reconsider their position. This seemed like a risky move, like rekindling an argument with your spouse a week after you've lost. But after Mims was rejected by the lower court and then the 11th Circuit appellate panel, the U.S. Supreme Court agreed to hear his case.

It looked like he might have a fighting chance in front of the Supremes. One of the Court's conservatives, Justice Samuel Alito, had already written an opinion in favor of Mims' position a few years earlier while serving in the 3rd Circuit. Alito had been outvoted in that case, but now he was in a position to impose his view on his former colleagues. Sweet revenge! Meanwhile, the liberal justices would certainly be happy to help someone who was challenging abusive practices by a corporation. It was the justices in the middle who were the troublesome ones, starting with Mr. Practical, Justice Stephen Breyer. This would become evident when the parties sent their lawyers to argue the case in person before the Court.

Breyer pointed out that the TCPA allowed lawsuits to be decided in small claims court without much hassle. But if a plaintiff had the option of filing in federal court instead, then a defendant could move a case there as well. This would stymie the ordinary bloke who was just trying to extract a few hundred bucks from a scofflaw telemarketer. Instead of a quick small claims judgment, he'd receive an intimidating letter informing him that his dispute has been transferred to the big downtown building with the $20/hour parking garage. The envelope would include a subpoena duces tecum, a writ of habeas corpus, and maybe even a gluteus maximus. Faced with paying thousands of dollars for lawyers, and missing a week of work for a stressful jury trial, he would give up on his quest for justice.

Mims' attorney, Scott Nelson, downplayed this possibility, calling it a "self-defeating" strategy that would cost the telemarketer far more than the potential damages at stake. However, Breyer and his fellow pragmatist, Justice Anthony Kennedy, were not persuaded. Breyer said:

> "If they're pests and they want to drag it out, what they do is they just remove it from small claims court. ... And so, what was Congress's objective, seemingly to provide a simple, clear, easy thing for the average American to do when he's pestered, suddenly becomes a major legal problem .... Now, that's something that's bothering me."

But Arrow's attorney, Gregory Garre, had the tougher argument to make. The default rule was that suits under federal law could be filed in either federal or state courts unless Congress said otherwise. The TCPA's private right of action said nothing that would explicitly overturn this rule. In fact, its language about "appropriate" state courts appeared to be unnecessary. Why would anyone sue in an *inappropriate* state court? To get the case dismissed, Garre had to convince the Supreme Court to read something into the law that wasn't there.

The justices weren't taking the bait. Instead, they took turns musing about the puzzling wording of the law. "I've never seen a statute remotely like this before," Chief Justice John Roberts remarked. "This is the strangest statute I've ever seen."

Justice Elena Kagan expressed a similar sentiment. "If both sides agree it's odd, and all nine justices agree it's odd, I mean, I think we can say this statute is odd."

By the time that oral arguments concluded, it was clear that the plaintiff had the upper hand. The TCPA may be odd, but Arrow's position would have made it even more of an oddity: a federal law that cannot be enforced in federal court. On January 18, 2012, the Court issued its ruling in an opinion written by Justice Ruth Ginsburg. The nine men and women had unanimously reached the conclusion that Mims could proceed with his claim.

For our hero from Florida, this decision led to a $40,000 judgment in his favor. For the rest of us, it firmly established that the TCPA wasn't just a toy for wannabe lawyers to piddle around with in small claims court. It was a powerful tool that could be used to unleash devastating punishment on companies—large and small—that failed to respect consumers' rights. And some interesting changes by Congress and the FCC had already expanded the reach of the original law, making it even more of a presence in Americans' lives. It is those changes that will be described in the next chapter.

4. THE CRACKDOWN OF 2003

When the TCPA was passed in 1991, its longest section was entitled "Protection of Subscriber Privacy Rights." This section rambled on for two and a half pages, just to tell the FCC to please start to think about possibly doing something to maybe let people opt out of receiving unsolicited telemarketing calls. It applied to both live telemarketing calls as well as robocalls, unlike the other parts of the law, but it wasn't exactly a clear mandate for action. This was all that was left of Representative Ed Markey's Do-Not-Call list proposal after the congressional negotiators and Direct Marketing Association lobbyists were done with it.

The FCC did study the issue as part of its rulemaking process in 1992, but the outcome was not what many citizens had hoped. Instead of implementing a Do-Not-Call list, the Commission provided a list of reasons why the idea was silly and impractical. The database of phone numbers would be costly to maintain, it said, with estimates in excess of $20 million per year and possibly even $80 million in the first year. It would be impossible to keep the list current when people's numbers change. There was no way to preserve confidentiality, and so unscrupulous companies would misuse the data. Also, those who sign up for the list would miss out on many enjoyable sales calls, since they couldn't specify which ones they might still want to receive. According to the FCC, the Do-Not-Call list was just plain wrong for America.

The Commission had sought comments on the Do-Not-Call idea, and only six consumer advocacy groups spoke out in favor of it. Meanwhile there were 25 trade associations, 17 common carriers, and 83 newspapers who were almost unanimously opposed. Inside the bubble of a federal agency, this is what passes for democracy. Even though the consumer groups were representing the interests of 250 million people, they were outvoted. As for the dozens of newspapers that wanted to continue their perpetual telemarketing campaigns, please keep them in mind whenever you hear someone bemoaning the death of print journalism. The dominance of biased cable TV news and internet reporting may signify a decline in editorial standards, but at least we no longer get relentless phone calls asking whether we want the *Pocono Bugle-Democrat-Gazette* thrown into our bushes six mornings each week.

Despite its desire to placate industry groups, the FCC couldn't completely ignore the problem of unrestrained telemarketing. It had to at least pretend to do something useful, and the solution it enacted in 1992 was the Company-Specific Do-Not-Call list. There was now a straightforward procedure to follow if a consumer wanted to avoid unsolicited calls. She could contact each of the thousands of businesses that sells products or services over the telephone, and ask for her phone number to be placed on that company's individual list. What could be easier?

In practice, however, the Company-Specific Do-Not-Call list proved to be completely inadequate. One reason is that we Americans are a lazy species, and we were getting even lazier in the 1990s. Few people were willing to invest two or three months of their time into notifying all of the local and national telemarketers to leave them alone. Instead, most folks waited until receiving an unwanted call from a particular business, and asked to be placed on the company's list at that moment. By then they had already been bothered, and it was too late.

Weak enforcement was another problem, because the private right of action is not as potent for the do-not-call provision as it is for robocalls and junk fax. A person cannot sue a company for disobeying the do-not-call rules until he or she has received at least two illegal calls within a twelve-month period. It's similar to the "one free bite" rule that is applied to vicious dogs. Additionally, this part of the TCPA does not impose strict liability. The offender can dodge the penalties by showing that he exercised "due care" and maintained "reasonable practices and procedures." Here, there is no analogous defense available to canines. A German shepherd isn't able to write a Human Interaction Compliance Manual and then later use it to excuse an unprovoked attack against the UPS guy.

The biggest concern, however, was that an invention from the late 1980s was greatly increasing the volume of telemarketing calls. At the same time, it was making them even more annoying. This invention was the predictive dialer.

Prior to the use of predictive dialers, call center agents would waste much of their day listening to busy signals, answering machine messages, and the endless ringing of unanswered phones.

But predictive dialing systems can place calls to multiple phone numbers at once, without routing any of the calls to an agent until the software detects that a live person is on the line. If someone answers the phone and there is no agent available to speak, the dialer can do one of two things: play a recorded message asking the recipient to wait, or simply disconnect the call. Since prerecorded messages are highly regulated by the TCPA, most predictive dialing systems do the latter.

When Caller ID became a standard phone feature in the 1990s, telemarketers and debt collectors discovered that fewer of their calls were being answered. They responded by relying more heavily on predictive dialers, and using them to place a larger number of simultaneous calls in an effort to keep all of their employees busy at all times. Even in the best of circumstances, a consumer who answered one of these calls would hear an awkward pause of several seconds before the dialing software connected him or her to an agent. But many times there would be just a pause and then a click as the system unceremoniously abandoned the call. This made it rather difficult for the recipient to ask to be added to the Company-Specific Do-Not-Call list, and so the same thing would often happen again the next day.

Public anger over excessive telemarketing, as well as the frequent hang-up calls from predictive dialers, caused the original Do-Not-Call list idea to resurface. Consumers in thirty-six states were able to sign up for these lists, but (as with the earlier battle against robocalls) it would require action at the national level to truly make a difference. This time it was the Federal Trade Commission (FTC) that would take the lead. In 1994, Congress had authorized the FTC to create rules against "deceptive" or "abusive" telemarketing practices. In 2002, the agency announced that it wanted to use that power to establish a national Do-Not-Call list. However, it first needed to go back to Congress and ask for something even more important than authority: money.

Congress was engaged in a divisive debate at this time about whether to invade Iraq. But telemarketers served as a unifying force among politicians of all stripes: they were now even less popular than Saddam Hussein. Capitalizing on the nation's mood, Representatives Billy Tauzin of Louisiana and John Dingell of Michigan introduced the bipartisan Do-Not-Call Implementation

Act. (Our old pal Ed Markey was one of the cosponsors.) It passed by a margin of 418-7 in the House of Representatives and a unanimous vote in the Senate. This bill called for the FTC to fund the Do-Not-Call list itself by collecting fees from telemarketers who needed to access the list. It also instructed the FCC and FTC to work together to ensure that the FCC's TCPA regulations and the FTC's Telemarketing Sales Rule were consistent. The fierce rivalry between these two agencies would have to be put on hold until the next time their softball teams played each other.

On March 11, 2003, President George W. Bush signed the act into law. Whatever his faults may have been, he was a savvier politician than his father. The elder Bush had signed the TCPA with little fanfare and more than a hint of displeasure. He acted as though he were approving a tax increase, or reluctantly selling the Grand Canyon to China to avert a national bankruptcy. But the younger Bush knew that the Do-Not-Call list was a proud achievement. In the summer of 2003, the president made a televised address from the White House rose garden to remind Americans to place their phone numbers on the list:

> "Unwanted telemarketing calls are intrusive, they are annoying, and they're all too common. When Americans are sitting down to dinner, or a parent is reading to his or her child, the last thing they need is a call from a stranger with a sales pitch."

Even the FCC, which had been so dismissive of the Do-Not-Call list a decade earlier, celebrated the moment. Its support was important because the FTC did not have jurisdiction over certain types of businesses, such as banks, airlines, and phone companies, and so the FCC would need to enact its own set of Do-Not-Call regulations to cover those entities. The FCC commissioners enthusiastically embraced this new tool in the fight against telephone spam. They noted that the cost of implementing the database in the first year was now estimated at $18.1 million, down significantly from the $80 million that had been predicted in 1992. This was credited primarily to improvements in computer technology. However, the more likely explanation for the discrepancy is that the earlier figure had been recklessly inflated in an effort to damage the proposal before it could even get off the ground.

The technical implementation of the Do-Not-Call database went smoothly, and over fifty million people signed up in the first few months. Telemarketers would be required to obey the new rules beginning on October 1. Although the public was eagerly awaiting the law, legal challenges by industry groups still stood in the way. A couple of surprising last minute court rulings nearly wrecked the Bush Administration's signature accomplishment.

On September 23, a judge in Oklahoma ruled that Congress had never granted the FTC any authority to oversee or enforce the Do-Not-Call list. This was a puzzling thing to say, given the overwhelming passage of the Do-Not-Call Implementation Act earlier in the year. However, the judge believed that the March law was merely an appropriation of money without the permission to do anything with it. Imagine someone giving you a dollar to buy a candy bar for them, but when you come back with the treat you are told that you hadn't been allowed to actually spend the cash. That's how the FTC felt, except that it wasn't even left with some candy that it could keep for itself. All it had was a database that would now be useless if the judge's opinion was allowed to stand.

Congress and the president understood the political peril that awaited them if all the hype about the Do-Not-Call list turned into a massive letdown. They sprung into action with uncharacteristic speed. On the day after the ruling, Tauzin and Dingell introduced a new bill to overcome the court's nitpicking and clarify that the FTC did, in fact, have the authority that Congress had intended to give it. This one didn't have a name, but it could have been called the "Yes, We Really Mean It Act." It passed the House by a vote of 412-8 and the Senate by 95-0. President Bush hurriedly signed it into law on September 29.

At this point, it's worth taking a quick look at the handful of misfit congressmen who ineffectually objected to one or both of the Do-Not-Call bills in 2003. Of these nine politicians, three would later run for president: Ron Paul, Tom Tancredo, and Tim Ryan. Two others—Ted Strickland and Jeff Flake—have also, at times, tried to position themselves for national office. The massive ego that it takes to oppose an overwhelmingly popular idea is certainly a helpful thing to have when launching a hopeless campaign for the presidency.

The more serious threat to the Do-Not-Call list came from a ruling by a Colorado federal court on September 25. Judge Edward Nottingham decreed that the list violated businesses' rights under the First Amendment. It failed the "reasonable fit" test from *Central Hudson* because the rules were under-inclusive: the FTC had unfairly restricted commercial telemarketing while exempting charitable fundraising calls. The judge didn't perceive any valid reason for this distinction:

> "Many a mountebank has utilized the corporate form, including nonprofit incorporation, to perpetrate fraud on unsuspecting consumers. In any type of transaction where money changes hands, whether charitable or commercial, fraudulent deeds will find a foothold and pose a risk to the public."

This was a convincing argument, and Nottingham scored extra points by skillfully resurrecting the forgotten word "mountebank." However, it was at odds with other court rulings that had upheld state versions of the Do-Not-Call list, and was unlikely to stand up on appeal. Nonetheless, Nottingham issued an injunction barring the FTC from enforcing its rules. In fact, the agency was ordered to completely suspend the operation of the database. No more consumers could sign up for the list, and no telemarketers could purchase access to it.

Now there was no amount of heroics by Congress or the president that could salvage the October 1 date. It had taken the FTC a year of tedious work and public hearings to draft its regulations, and expanding them to cover calls by non-profit organizations couldn't be done in five or six days. Repealing the First Amendment in that time span was just as daunting. The best hope was that there might be good news from the battlefront in Iraq to take Americans' minds off of the issue until the ruling could be appealed.

Fortunately, the Colorado ruling caused only a short delay. The 10th Circuit Court of Appeals lifted the injunction on October 7, allowing the Do-Not-Call list to take effect while they studied the issue more closely. In the following February, they overturned Nottingham's decision. They decided that it was acceptable for the FTC to give non-profit groups an exemption, because:

> "[A] significant purpose of the call is to sell a cause, not merely to receive a donation, and ... non-commercial callers thus have stronger incentives not to alienate the people they call or to engage in abusive and deceptive practices."

The cloud of unconstitutionality was lifted. The telemarketers made one last ditch appeal to the Supreme Court, but the justices refused to hear the case. The Do-Not-Call list was here to stay.

Even before all the appeals were settled, Americans were celebrating. People who had signed up for the list were instantly noticing the difference that the law had made. Their phones were no longer ringing every night with offers for newspaper subscriptions and home improvement services. It was a rare government success story, and the credit could rightly be shared among Congress, President Bush, the FTC, and the FCC. Some of the accolades also went to AT&T, which had successfully delivered the computer software for the project. It was a cruel irony when, only a month later, the FCC announced that it was fining AT&T the amount of $780,000 for repeatedly violating the Company-Specific Do-Not-Call rules. (The corporation would ultimately settle the charges by paying $490,000.)

But the Do-Not-Call list was only the most visible part of the crackdown. Both the FTC and the FCC were also eager to address the problems being caused by predictive dialers. Even when this type of equipment is used correctly, occasional nuisance hang-up calls are inevitable. It isn't a defect; it's by design. However, some homes were receiving as many as ten or twenty of these disconnects a day from various companies. That seemed like just a little too much, and it was prompting complaints to the government.

The agencies briefly pondered a total ban on predictive dialers, but several industry groups argued that this would reduce call center efficiency and force companies to hire more people. Obviously, that was a non-starter. So the FTC and FCC settled on a compromise rule that was intended to mitigate, but not eliminate, the hang-ups. Among other restrictions, they set a numeric limit on disconnected calls. Telemarketers would now be required to transfer 97% of calls to live agents within two seconds after the recipient answers. The other 3% of calls could be abandoned after playing a brief recorded message.

This complex regulation is tricky to obey, and is even more difficult to enforce. That's why it was imposed only on commercial telemarketing campaigns, which were about to be severely hobbled by the new Do-Not-Call list anyway. There aren't many similarly constructed rules for the rest of society. What if we were allowed to ignore 3% of the traffic lights that we encounter, or give a karate-style kick to 3% of the people who annoy us? It might be fun at first, but the record-keeping would quickly become tedious.

There was one other big rule change in 2003, and it proved to be perhaps the most consequential and controversial of all. As mentioned earlier, the TCPA puts restrictions on autodialed calls to cell phones, emergency lines, and hospital rooms. Roughly two-thirds of Americans now owned mobile phones. Now that predictive dialers had also become commonplace, and had revealed themselves to be problematic, there was a question as to whether or not they qualified as automatic dialing equipment. If they did, then companies would need to get permission before using them to call wireless numbers.

The actual phrase used in the TCPA is "automatic telephone dialing system," often abbreviated in legal documents as "ATDS." Congress had provided a definition as part of the law:

> "The term 'automatic telephone dialing system' means equipment which has the capacity to store or produce telephone numbers to be called, using a random or sequential number generator; and to dial such numbers."

There were a couple types of dialers that everyone agreed were covered by this definition. For example, a robocalling machine that dials every number in a telephone exchange is clearly an ATDS. Of course, these kinds of machines also deliver prerecorded messages, so it's usually illegal to call cell phone numbers with them anyway.

The 1983 hit movie *WarGames* provided another obvious example of an ATDS. In that film, the lead character was a spoiled teenage snot played by a non-teenager named Matthew Broderick.

(By the time Broderick portrayed an even more spoiled teen in *Ferris Bueller's Day Off*, a few years later, he was nearing eligibility for an AARP membership.) The *WarGames* protagonist used a personal computer and modem to sequentially dial phone numbers while looking for other computer systems that he could hack. The movie gave rise to the term "war dialing" to describe this activity. The kid in the film almost started World War III, but war dialers in the real world are mostly used for locating fax machines to target with advertising. Hollywood chose to slightly exaggerate the threat so that it would be a more compelling story, since no one would have paid $4 to see a movie about junk fax.

Most predictive dialers are different from these types of devices, since they work from a list of known telephone numbers that is loaded into the machine at the start of each shift. There is no random or sequential generation of the numbers. Prior to 2003, there was an implicit belief that list-based dialers were outside the reach of the TCPA.

But when the FCC studied the matter more closely, it focused on a particular word from the ATDS definition: "capacity." A predictive dialer certainly has the capacity to store and automatically dial every phone number in an exchange, even if it is operating from a list. All that it takes is to load those 10,000 numbers into the system. Furthermore, it can behave in an aggressive and annoying manner, by placing multiple calls at once and hanging up on people when there aren't enough agents available. The Commission quickly determined that a rule clarification was needed:

> "[T]o exclude from these restrictions equipment that use predictive dialing software ... simply because it relies on a given set of numbers would lead to an unintended result. Calls to emergency numbers, health care facilities, and wireless numbers would be permissible when the dialing equipment is paired with predictive dialing software and a database of numbers, but prohibited when the equipment operates independently of such lists and software packages. ... [T]he Commission finds that a predictive dialer falls within the meaning and statutory definition of 'automatic telephone dialing equipment' and the intent of Congress."

So, there were some new restrictions on the types of systems that could be used to call mobile phones. This posed a bit of a problem, because phone number portability was also being implemented in 2003. It would now be possible for landline phone numbers to be converted to cell phone service or back again. Organizations that used robocalls or predictive dialers would need to subscribe to an online database that provided daily updates on which phone numbers were now off limits. But many companies either didn't know about the database, or considered the rules too costly and burdensome to follow. Some would later pay a price that could be measured in lawsuits and bad publicity.

The Commission was proud of its new regulations, and proceeded to take a victory lap. Chairman Michael Powell issued a statement. "Our decision today is the most sweeping consumer protection measure ever adopted by the FCC," he said. "Taken together and combined with vigilant enforcement, our rules provide consumers with the tools they need to craft the commercial relationships they want." The other commissioners also expressed their satisfaction with the work they had done together, and with the cooperation they had received from the FTC. Maybe next year's inter-agency softball game would feature fewer beanballs than usual.

Indeed, the 2003 version of the FCC had done a respectable job of balancing the concerns of everyday Americans with the First Amendment rights of businesses. However, it declined to revisit the loophole for most landline robocalls that it had enacted in 1992. This would lead to disillusionment within a few years, as people began to question why they were still getting these calls despite signing up for the Do-Not-Call list. And the "vigilant enforcement" promised by Powell would fail to materialize when some of the unwanted robocalls began to illegally follow consumers to their cellular phones.

The Do-Not-Call list did succeed in silencing many of the unwanted calls from legitimate telemarketers. For the next few years, the main telephone nuisances would be robocallers with nothing useful to sell: political organizations, non-profit fundraisers, and—the worst-behaved of all—bill collectors. These groups were exempt from the Do-Not-Call list and from the TCPA's rule against robocalls to home phones. They will be the focus of the next three chapters.

5. POLITICAL ROBOCALLS: ONE MORE REASON NOT TO VOTE

Politics isn't just a world of riches and glamour. Some elected officials have low-paid, thankless jobs that no sane person would enjoy, like school board member or town ombudsman. Thankfully, there are many patriotic citizens in our communities who routinely offer to fall on the sword of public service and seek these positions. The least we can do is listen to what these unselfish men and women say when they campaign for our votes.

At one time, robocalls may have been a good way for these candidates to tell us about themselves. But dark money from mysterious groups with undisclosed donors has contributed to a decrease in the quality and truthfulness of all forms of political messaging over the past few decades. Robocalls are no exception. As an example, let's take a look at a typical prerecorded call from thirty years ago:

"Hi, I'm Frank Popinjay, your county supervisor for District Three. I'm proud of my service to Magoo County these past four years. Under my leadership we finally paved Turkeypie Road, and we plugged the dangerous open well that had swallowed up three of our county's children. We even extended sewer service to the southern end of the county. Remember that big ol' stink from the overflowing septic tank at Josh Winmore's farm? Now Josh has a sewer and his neighbors can breathe easy again. I'm asking for your vote on November 6 so that we can continue the progress. Thank you, and God bless."

That call was paid for by Frank Popinjay and his loving wife Phyllis. It has some folksy appeal, but it's no match for the types of robocalls made more recently:

"This is Americans for Enterprise and Religious Liberty with an important message about Frank Popinjay. Popinjay and his cronies spent *your* money on a sewer that funnels disease, drugs, and illegal immigration underneath Magoo County. Popinjay even billed the taxpayers $679 for his luxury trip to meet with Big Plumbing fat cats in Kohler, Wisconsin. It's time to flush Popinjay's brand of sewer politics. Vote for change in District Three this November."

Who paid for that message? Most likely, it's an anonymous billionaire who will never set foot in Magoo County. He's playing a global game of chess against other billionaires, and the defeat of Frank Popinjay will help him gain some tiny, momentary advantage. Plus, he's the type of person who likes hearing about children falling down wells, and he's still pissed that Frank took that enjoyment away from him.

Now, however, the cost of robocalls has dropped so far that anyone can afford them. They are no longer the exclusive tool of selfish rich guys, because someone else has embraced the technology: racist poor guys. Any white supremacist association can use $200 of its meth lab profits to offend thousands of people in a distant state. When you see an unfamiliar Idaho phone number on your Caller ID, you know you're about to endure a dose of end-stage democracy from some group with three members that has "Aryan" in its name. Either that, or you forgot to pay the potato bill again.

Legislators in some states have attempted to outlaw political robocalls, or place restrictions on them that don't apply to other types of calls. These lawmakers should be required to read Chapter 3 of this book. Singling out one type of speech based on its content, especially when it is non-commercial speech, is almost always a violation of the First Amendment. The only successful bans are those that are part of broader laws against all categories of unsolicited prerecorded calls. Minnesota and Indiana have figured this out; most other states have not.

If you don't live in one of the enlightened states, one way of reining in this type of nuisance is to drop your landline and port the number to a cell phone. The TCPA's rules against automated calls to wireless phone numbers are content-neutral, and restrict political robocalls just like any others. However, some politicians (and their campaign consultants) have difficulty accepting that there is a law that applies to them. This means that even cell phones will get an occasional political robocall.

Theoretically, you can sue and recover damages from political groups that violate the TCPA, just like you can from telemarketers and debt collectors. However, the typical campaign fund disbands shortly after Election Day, so there is only a short window to cash in. Plus, some candidates use their money irresponsibly and finish in the red. If your cell phone happens to get an illegal robocall from the William Weld for President Campaign Committee, you better hurry up and collect your $500 before it is spent on a doubly misnamed "Victory Celebration."

Members of Congress have a particularly bad reputation for disobeying the TCPA. One of the worst examples of this occurred in 2009, when Texas Representatives Lamar Smith and Mike Conaway were both caught making tens of thousands of unlawful automated calls to constituents' cell phones. As if this weren't disappointing enough, they used taxpayer money to pay for the calls. The *Austin American-Statesman* noted that the FCC could, in theory, fine Smith's congressional office $2.31 billion (roughly 1,500 times his annual budget). Luckily for the taxpayers, who would have also been stuck with the fine, the FCC chose not to do so.

The embarrassed congressmen immediately apologized and accepted full responsibility for the incident. They reimbursed the government for the cost of the illegal calling campaigns, and offered to pay the phone bills of anyone who had incurred extra charges. Both men then resigned from office in shame and vowed to lead more virtuous lives in the private sector.

If you believed anything in the last paragraph, you don't know very much about American politics. What really happened is that staff members for the congressmen faulted the Congressional Franking Commission (CFC) for wrongly approving the calls. The CFC's responsibility, however, is limited to reviewing the wording of messages—not the delivery. While their assistants deflected the blame, Smith and Conaway laid low for a while until the scandal was forgotten.

Robocalls from congressmen and congresswomen have continued to be a problem, due to the invention of the "telephone town hall." This is a way for politicians to interact with their constituents without being booed or having shoes thrown at them. It's actually a good idea if done correctly as an opt-in meeting. Those who want to participate can sign up for the tele-town hall in advance, and then they can be called when it is about to begin. Unfortunately, some members of Congress haven't yet realized that they are not the center of the universe. They insist on phoning *everyone* in their district at the start of each town hall, which is usually around dinner time. Few people want to hear some egotistical dullard bloviate about health care reform while their family is neck deep in a bucket of fried chicken.

These tele-town halls and similar messages from politicians recently became harder to avoid, due to a remarkably convoluted sequence of events that had little to do with politics. It all began on May 10, 2006. On that fateful day, Jose Gomez of California received this text message on his phone:

"Destined for something big? Do it in the navy. Get a career. An education. And a chance to serve a greater cause. For a FREE Navy video call 1-800-510-2074."

Many people who get a message like this will immediately begin to fantasize about what life would be like in the United States Navy. They will call for their free video, talk to a recruiter, and pass a physical examination that involves crawling around on their knees in their underwear. Then they will spend the next four years traveling the world, learning new technologies, and defending freedom. But some people won't have the same reaction. They will instead spend the next four years stewing in anger that a telemarketer has violated their rights—and besmirched the Navy's good name—by sending them a spam text. Can you guess which category Jose Gomez was in?

The Navy's advertising campaign was managed by the highly respected Campbell-Ewald Company. Campbell-Ewald had delegated the text messaging to its subcontractor MindMatics, which boasted of having a list of three million people who had asked to receive ads such as these. Of these, roughly 150,000 were males ages 18 to 24, and they would be the ones targeted with the messages. It was astounding that so many people were willing to allow solicitations to be broadcast to their phones while getting nothing in return. Yet, Campbell-Ewald didn't ask too many questions about how this supposed "opt-in" list was assembled. It would later regret not doing so.

In reality, Gomez had never asked MindMatics to send him text messages about military service. Plus, he was almost forty years old. If the Navy relied on MindMatics' list for recruiting, it was going to get a bunch of middle-aged sailors who moan about their arthritis every time they are told to swab the poop deck. It was also going to risk running afoul of the law.

As part of its 2003 ruling, the FCC had opined that text messages delivered to wireless phones were the same thing as "calls" under the TCPA. But not everyone was persuaded that the Commission's interpretation would hold up in court. Even if it did, there might be some clever ways to get around the rule. For example, some telemarketers sent mass emails that were converted into mass texts, under the belief that the TCPA was inapplicable to email. The relevant law would instead be the CAN-SPAM Act. This law means exactly what the name says: you *can spam* people via email, and there is little they can do to stop you. The CAN-SPAM Act's private right of action is so weak that it might as well be made of soggy tissues. Only internet service providers can sue an email spammer, and only when they have suffered devastating harm to their networks. The mere receipt of a spam email, or of a thousand spam emails, confers no right to recover damages.

While Gomez was seething about the Navy's misguided recruiting attempt, courts were considering various TCPA cases involving text spam. The interpretation of the law was evolving in favor of the consumer, and marketers' attempts to shield themselves with the CAN-SPAM Act were being pushed aside. Probably the most influential decision was the *Satterfield* ruling of 2009 by the 9th Circuit Court of Appeals. This lawsuit was brought by a woman who had downloaded a free ringtone for her young son. Her information was then sold to a telemarketer who sent an unwanted text message promoting Stephen King's novels. (Maybe King's books would be good to read to her child, to teach him to avoid rabid dogs, haunted cars, and homicidal clowns.) The 9th Circuit decided in her favor on all relevant issues: a text was a "call" under the TCPA, mass texting equipment may qualify as an "automatic telephone dialing system," and she hadn't given consent to receive the message.

Emboldened by the *Satterfield* opinion, Gomez filed a TCPA lawsuit just prior to the expiration of the statute of limitations in

2010. However, he didn't want to sue the Navy, since it would certainly claim to have sovereign immunity. Plus, he might need it to rescue him from pirates someday. He also couldn't sue MindMatics, because by this time it was "judgment proof." That's a polite way of saying it had been involved in enough other screw-ups that it didn't have any assets left for Gomez to take. But Campbell-Ewald could be held liable for MindMatics' error under the doctrine of vicarious liability, and it had deep pockets. It was the only defendant that was needed.

Since his case involved only one text message, and a penalty of $500 to $1,500, it wasn't economical for Gomez to pursue it on an individual basis. He instead filed it as a class action on behalf of the 150,000 people who received a similar text. This would allow his legal fees to be shared among everyone who claimed a piece of the award, but it also greatly raised the stakes. There wasn't going to be a quick and sarcastic verdict from Judge Judy. Instead, it would be scorched earth litigation warfare.

Campbell-Ewald was facing a potential loss of over $200 million for a four-year-old text message that it hadn't even sent. Its lawyers had two strategies for dealing with this crisis. One was to argue that the company inherited the Navy's sovereign immunity, since it was carrying out a government contract. The other was to offer to settle with Gomez for slightly more than the maximum amount of his personal claim: $1,503 plus costs.

The company knew that Gomez would reject the offer, since accepting it would end the class action portion of the case immediately. Without also collecting damages for the thousands of Navy text messages sent to other people, the payout for Gomez's one illegal text would not be nearly enough to cover his attorneys' bills. (The "costs" included in the offer were for things like court fees, expert witnesses, and deposition expenses—not lawyers.) However, Campbell-Ewald hoped that the existence of the offer would compel the court to dismiss the case. Why hold a trial when the defendant has already capitulated and agreed to give the plaintiff everything that he is entitled to get? Plus $3 for a cup of coffee!

Both of these strategies proved to be extremely contentious. The lawsuit dragged on for years, with points being scored on each side, before landing in the U.S. Supreme Court on October 14, 2015. Campbell-Ewald didn't spare any expense here. They hired the one and only attorney who had previously defended a TCPA case in oral arguments before the Court: Gregory Garre. *Mims* had been a loss for Garre, but that was no reflection on his abilities. In fact, he had once served as the solicitor general for the United States—a position that has also been occupied by Thurgood Marshall, Ken Starr, and Elena Kagan. He was, and still is, one of the elites of the Washington legal world.

The argument in the Supreme Court focused almost exclusively on whether the $1,503 offer was sufficient to end the lawsuit. This was a highly technical matter involving a fine point of civil procedure, but it yielded some strong opinions. The more liberal justices were exasperated by Campbell-Ewald's position. The company had dictated the terms of a settlement agreement, which Gomez refused to sign, and then had arrogantly insisted that it was somehow a binding contract. Furthermore, the money hadn't actually been paid. What if Campbell-Ewald decided to renege after the suit was dismissed? It was an unlikely possibility, but this case had already had its share of unlikely turns.

The conservatives were equally frustrated, but for a different reason. Why wouldn't Gomez just accept the damn offer and stop wasting everyone's time? Obviously, he and his lawyers were hoping to recover all of their litigation expenses and fees, which were by now approaching the cost of a space shuttle mission. However, the TCPA's private right of action was written with small claims court in mind, and it does not allow for attorneys' fees to be awarded to the prevailing party. Gomez was holding out for something that he couldn't have. Justice Antonin Scalia wondered what other unreasonable demands a plaintiff could use as an excuse for rejecting a generous settlement.

"I suppose he could ask for the key to Fort Knox, right?" Scalia asked. "And then no settlement offer would suffice, right?"

"He could ask for a unicorn, your honor," Garre replied.

Scalia agreed. "He could ask for a unicorn."

When the Court issued its opinion on January 20, 2016, Justice Ginsburg once again had bad news to deliver to Garre. The Court decided, by a margin of 6-3, that the company's unaccepted settlement offer to Gomez was unenforceable, no matter how munificent it may have been. This ruling made it harder for defendants to avoid costly class actions by "picking off" the lead plaintiffs. It would have an impact on the TCPA and beyond.

But it was the Court's decision on sovereign immunity—a topic that had barely been discussed during oral arguments—that may ultimately prove more consequential. The justices agreed with Campbell-Ewald that the federal government could not be sued under the TCPA. It also agreed that contractors acquire "derivative" immunity from the government when they are merely doing what they are told. However, the Navy had ordered the text messages to be sent only to people on an opt-in list. When the advertisement was texted to Gomez, who had not given his consent, MindMatics and Campbell-Ewald exceeded the scope of the contract. Under these circumstances, derivative sovereign immunity was not a defense.

It was a clear victory for Gomez, but by this time nearly ten years had elapsed since the offending text message campaign. It would be a herculean challenge to locate most of the victims who might be entitled to a portion of a class settlement. So, the parties simply agreed to settle the case without involving the other potential class members. The details were not disclosed, but we can surmise that the plaintiff used the threat of continuing with the class action to extract favorable terms. His attorneys presumably received some compensation for their many hours of work, even though the TCPA doesn't say that a plaintiff can recover these fees. And Gomez himself was probably eating unicorn sandwiches for weeks.

Although this case was a win for one individual consumer, there was a dark cloud buried in the silver lining. The Supreme Court's discussion of sovereign immunity compelled the FCC to reconsider one of its positions. Ever since the Texas scandal in 2009, the Commission had been reminding members of Congress that they were obligated to obey the TCPA's restrictions on automated calls to cell phones. But now the Court was saying something different: the federal government and its branches, agencies, and representatives are immune from this law, and so are any contractors that correctly do the government's bidding. So, the FCC was forced to issue a declaratory ruling shortly after the *Gomez* decision, reversing its previous guidance. If a congressman wants to robocall constituents as part of his supposed official responsibilities, there is now nothing stopping him from calling both landlines and cell phones without permission. The dreaded telephone town halls are back on the dinnertime agenda.

This raises two unresolved concerns that are far more worrisome than an occasional ruined meal. First, if members of Congress have sovereign immunity, what about other officials? Can state legislators, governors, and county tax clerks also robocall our cell phones with "government performance updates" in which they tell us about their accomplishments? Can the president call to brag about his inauguration crowd size if, hypothetically, he were the sort of immodest person who would do so? If so, let's hope that no one figures this out any time soon. We don't need a robocall from the mayor each time a pothole gets fixed.

The second, and more serious, problem is that this exception throws the constitutionality of the TCPA back into doubt. The First Amendment doesn't allow laws to discriminate against political speech based on its viewpoint. If an incumbent officeholder is permitted to promote himself with calls that would otherwise be illegal, his opponents have a plausible argument for demanding equal time. Why shouldn't they be allowed to break the law too? This type of dispute could degenerate into chaos, and eventually force all legal constraints to be lifted on political robocalls and bulk text messages. And it's all because a Navy subcontractor botched a recruitment campaign in 2006.

There is one other type of political robocall that must be discussed in this chapter: the dirty trick. This often involves some kind of misattribution, in which the caller falsely claims to be associated with his opponent's campaign. One of the most successful robocalls of this kind occurred in a place that isn't usually associated with nasty politics or corruption. It wasn't New Jersey, and it wasn't Chicago or Louisiana. It wasn't even this author's old 8th grade classroom at a Catholic school in Kentucky, where the student government elections were routinely rigged by an elderly nun. This dirty robocall campaign happened during a congressional race in the peaceful corn fields of western Nebraska, and the target was Scott Kleeb.

Kleeb was a dream candidate: a young, charismatic man who had, quite improbably, acquired a Ph.D. from Yale despite dressing like a cowboy and working on a ranch. He was a Democrat running in a Republican district, but this was 2006 and President Bush was no longer basking in the glory that the Do-Not-Call list had brought him. Indeed, Bush's popularity had sunk so far that it threatened to undo the GOP's hold on safe congressional seats such as the Nebraska Third. As Election Day neared, Kleeb appeared to have a slight advantage.

But then came a last minute barrage of mysterious robocalls. "Hi, this is Scott Kleeb," they began, using part of a recording taken from one of Kleeb's own calls. The rest of the message proceeded to advocate a number of unpopular positions. By the time each call was finished, the recipient would believe that Kleeb was an out-of-touch egghead who wanted to eliminate farm subsidies, bulldoze state landmarks like Chimney Rock and Carhenge, and root for Texas A&M at the next Cornhuskers football game. Worse still, many people got repeated calls in the middle of the night, with Caller ID numbers manipulated to suggest that they had actually come from the Democrat's campaign. At this late stage of the race, there was no way to recover. Down went the Kleebster.

The Nebraska Public Service Commission investigated the calls for months, hoping to issue a fine for violating the state's autodialer registration rules, but was never able to determine who was to blame. (It was probably the Republicans, but the commissioners apparently didn't think of that.) Kleeb expressed disappointment that the guilty would go unpunished, and that Nebraskans' faith in the election process had been shaken. However, if he hadn't already sent out a few annoying robocalls himself, the impostor calls wouldn't have been so believable.

In some instances, a dirty trick can do collateral damage to people who aren't even involved in a race. This happened in Missouri in 2010 when a series of robocalls went out all across the state, using faked Caller ID information from local hospitals and ambulance services. When answered, the calls declared, "This is an urgent alert!" Many people assumed that a family member had been injured or killed, so they stayed on the line to hear the bad news. The message then proceeded to inform them, rather inaccurately, that one of their local legislative candidates had been involved with the "hard-core pornography industry."

St. Luke's Hospital, in the Kansas City area, was inundated with calls from people who had seen the hospital's number on their Caller ID. Many of the callers were outraged about the offensive and defamatory messages they had received. Others probably just wanted to know where they could buy some of the hard-core pornography. The hospital needed to reallocate staff to handle all of the inquiries and complaints. Its lawyers soon tracked down the source of the robocalls: a one-man political consulting firm operating from a house in the suburbs of St. Louis. The "company"—if you can call it that—agreed to stop spoofing the hospital's number and reimburse it $6,000 for its legal expenses.

One of the most frequently disrespected sections of the TCPA is entitled "Technical and Procedural Standards." It requires all robocallers to identify themselves at the start of each call, and they must also include their phone number somewhere in the message. Most political dirty tricksters break this rule, and usually they get away with it. The FCC has shown little interest in enforcing the identification requirements, and the TCPA's private right of action is not available for this offense. Therefore, prosecution is normally left up to the attorneys general of the fifty states, who pursue only the most outrageous violators.

In January 2006, an anonymous robocalling campaign shattered a peaceful Sunday afternoon in Oklahoma City. It was an automated telephone survey regarding one of the county commissioners. The message asked whether the commissioner "should continue using his position to advance the homosexual agenda." The recipients were told to press "1" for yes or "2" for no. It's unclear which option was more popular, and whether this was intended to be a binding referendum.

After receiving nine complaints, the state attorney general's office began investigating the calls. The best clue to the caller's identity was that the message used the word "homosexual" five times in about 40 seconds. Clearly, the robocalls were sponsored by someone who was thoroughly obsessed with, and perhaps even fascinated by, homosexuality. The A.G. could have done some sleuthing to find out who in the Oklahoma City area was watching that *Queer Eye* show for hours at a time. Instead, he obtained the dialing records for some of the calls. The evidence led him to the perpetrator: a happily married heterosexual man who had once served as a conservative member of the Oklahoma legislature. Sometimes it's the person you least suspect.

The attorney general estimated that 20,000 illegal calls had been made, and that half of those were answered. He was a compassionate man, however, and he gave the defendant a major break. The fine would be only $100 for each answered call, instead of the $500 (or more) that was specified by the TCPA. The former legislator could simply write a $1 million check and then be done with the matter, but he instead decided to fight the penalty in court. He raised a novel First Amendment defense, claiming that the TCPA was infringing on his constitutional rights by requiring him to identify himself in his prerecorded messages. After all, anonymous political speech was a patriotic American tradition dating back to the Revolutionary War era. This man didn't deserve to be fined for his "homosexual agenda" survey; he deserved a spot next to Thomas Paine in the history books.

The judge wasn't very impressed by the constitutional argument, but she also wasn't convinced that the attorney general's call volume estimates were accurate. She chose to issue a penalty of $500 for each of the nine sworn complaints that had been filed. It was a far cry from what the A.G. had proposed, but still enough to hurt. That $4,500 could have paid for the caller to see a few female impersonator revues in Vegas as part of his (ahem) "research."

But there is one anonymous political robocall that backfired more sensationally than any other. In the 2010 election, Maryland's previous governor Bob Ehrlich was in a rematch against the man who had defeated him four years earlier, Martin O'Malley. The odds were not in Ehrlich's favor. As a conservative Republican in a Democratic state, he needed more than just a strong debate performance, perfect hair, and an endorsement from Who-Gives-a-Crap on the opinion pages of the *Baltimore Sun*. He also needed to broaden his appeal beyond his base, which seemed to consist mainly of one or two white families in a mountain village outside of Cumberland. So, his campaign hired a consulting firm owned by an African-American Democrat, Julius Henson.

Henson did some routine work for Ehrlich in the weeks leading up to November, but saved his biggest effort for the afternoon and evening of Election Day. Several hours before the polls closed, he robocalled 112,000 urban and suburban Democratic voters with this message:

"Hello. I'm calling to let everyone know that Governor O'Malley and President Obama have been successful. Our goals have been met. The polls were correct and we took it back. We're OK. Relax. Everything is fine. The only thing left is to watch it on TV tonight. Congratulations and thank you."

Democrats were outraged by this obvious attempt at suppression. The party didn't want its supporters to relax and watch TV until after all the ballots were cast. Even if they already voted, they should head back to the precinct and vote again.

Henson had a different opinion: this was one of the cleanest robocalls in the history of politics. For one thing, it was entirely positive. Instead of calling O'Malley a "doodyhead" or accusing him of cannibalism, it thanked and congratulated his supporters. Also, it turned out to be highly accurate. The polls were indeed correct, O'Malley was winning re-election by a comfortable margin, and 112,000 Democrats could stay home (or even switch sides) without affecting the outcome. Most Marylanders thought Bob Ehrlich was doing an outstanding job as ex-governor, and they wanted him to continue in that role indefinitely.

Regardless of whether the call was ethical, it certainly wasn't legal. The state attorney general sued Henson and his firm for disobeying the TCPA's technical and procedural standards. Henson's employee, whose voice was heard on the message, admitted that she and her boss were both aware that the calls were missing the mandatory disclosures of the caller's name and phone number. Therefore, each call was a willful and knowing violation which could result in a $1,500 penalty. The total damages could exceed $162 million.

Although the usual First Amendment defenses were raised, the Eighth Amendment's protection against "excessive fines" proved to be more important. The judge reduced the penalty until she felt it was reasonable under the circumstances. Ultimately, Henson and his firm were made to pay $1 million. His employee was also fined $10,000 for her part in recording the message.

Additionally, the calls didn't comply with state election laws which require each political message to announce who had paid for it. This was a criminal offense. Henson served thirty days in jail, quite bitterly, and Ehrlich's campaign manager spent thirty days in home detention for participating in the conspiracy. (The ex-governor himself denied knowing anything about it.) The Great Chesapeake Caper of 2010 remains one of very few incidents in which someone has been imprisoned for making a robocall.

In most cases, political phone spam is a temporary autumn nuisance. It strikes us hard for a few weeks, like a plague of locusts or a bout with bronchitis, and then vanishes as quickly as it came. But the majority of robocalls are looking for money, not votes, and greed is always in season. Greed will be the topic of the next chapter. And the one after that. And pretty much the rest of the book.

6. LONG DISTANCE PANHANDLERS

Not every dime that we give to a non-profit group will be used for noble deeds. This is especially true when money is pledged over the phone. Telemarketing companies who work on behalf of charities will usually take the lion's share of the proceeds—often around 85%. And that's not counting the charity's internal costs related to the fundraising campaign, such as hiring a public relations team to undo the reputational damage caused by all the bothersome begging.

Even the 15% or so of the funds that make it past the telemarketer aren't always spent as we intend them to be. For example, consider the numerous police groups who solicit over the phone. These are very popular, because everybody seems to have a soft spot for our boys in blue. The typical donor expects his money to be used on beneficial things like bulletproof vests, scholarships for criminal justice majors, and legal fees to defend the nearsighted cop who thought a guy using a weed-eater was actually brandishing an M16. Instead, a lot of this cash is spent on "fraternal activities" such as banquets, awards presentations, and golf outings. Some groups even use it for political lobbying on issues of interest to law enforcement. When you can't get the natural cure that you need for your sleep apnea, you can blame your state's police associations for defeating the medical marijuana proposal that everyone else supported.

It's easy to think of a few rules that could fix the chronic problem of misdirected donations. Perhaps for-profit telemarketing firms should only be allowed to keep a small portion of any charitable proceeds that they raise? Or maybe solicitors should be required to warn potential donors that just a tiny sliver of their cash will be spent on anything worthwhile? In fact, laws like this used to exist in many states and localities. To understand why there are no such regulations today, we'll need to first travel back in time to the 1970s. That's when the environmental justice group Citizens for a Better Environment (CBE) was launched, with a goal of educating the public and policymakers about the dangerous effects of pollution on lower income neighborhoods.

CBE employed a team of door-to-door canvassers who fanned out across the Chicago area, explaining to residents how the air and water of northern Illinois were slowly poisoning everyone. They also asked for donations so that they could continue this outreach campaign. Everything was going well until CBE's representatives arrived in the Village of Schaumburg. Before the village would issue a solicitation permit, it required the group to prove that it spent at least 75% of donations on its stated charitable purpose. Money spent on fundraising and administration did not count. Most groups would find it difficult to meet this 75% standard, and CBE was no exception.

Schaumburg's permit rules were very meddlesome and more than a little arbitrary. For example, CBE's canvassers weren't just asking for money; they were spreading the environmental gospel. Yet, the village considered them to merely be fundraisers whose wages weren't tallied toward the 75% requirement. CBE had also hired a staff of research scientists, but Schaumburg thought that this type of expenditure didn't directly advance the group's mission of environmental education. It might be OK to print pamphlets discouraging people from discarding used motor oil in their neighbor's koi pond. It wasn't OK to use donations to pay a bunch of geeks to dork around with dioxin in a laboratory.

CBE challenged the constitutionality of the permit rule, and in 1980 it won a victory in the U.S. Supreme Court. By an 8-1 margin, with Justice William Rehnquist the only hold-out, the Court ruled that Schaumburg had violated the group's free speech rights. Begging for cash was protected by the First Amendment, and in this case it was also intertwined with issue advocacy. If the village wanted to place conditions on this activity, its rules had to be narrowly tailored to advance an important government interest. Schaumburg's ordinance, however, was overly broad and nearly impossible to comply with.

A similar case reached the Court a few years later, but this time the petitioner's motives weren't so pure. The Joseph H. Munson Company was in the business of raising money for non-profit organizations such as the Fraternal Order of Police (F.O.P.). Maryland had enacted a law limiting professional fundraisers to a fee of 25%, which in Munson's view was not nearly enough. If the F.O.P. wanted donations it should have to pay dearly for them. The company challenged the law's constitutionality, claiming that it violated its own right to free speech and the F.O.P.'s right to be gouged.

Maryland's law differed from the Schaumburg ordinance in two important ways. First, it targeted only fundraising expenses, and didn't make moral judgments about other types of administrative costs that a charity might incur. And second, if a non-profit organization couldn't find a solicitor who would work for only a 25% commission, it could get a waiver to hire someone else. It appeared that the state had found a way to negate the Supreme Court's concerns from the CBE case, and its law had a good chance of being upheld.

However, the Court found that Maryland's law was overly broad, just like Schaumburg's. The state had a compelling interest in preventing fraud, but an arbitrary limit on fundraising costs can have a "chilling" effect on honest organizations as well as dishonest ones. Rehnquist was once again on the losing side, albeit by only a 5-4 margin, and this time he was irked. To him, the law wasn't even about speech, nor was it necessarily about fraud. It was a simple economic regulation designed to protect both charities and the public. In his dissenting opinion, he said that the Court had missed the point of what the state was trying to achieve:

> "The concern is not that someone may abscond to South America with the funds collected. Rather, a high fundraising fee itself betrays the expectations of the donor who thinks that his money will be used to benefit the charitable purpose in the name of which the money was solicited."

It was a third Supreme Court ruling that would remove nearly all remaining constraints on the telemarketing companies that were collecting unconscionable fees. In the *Riley* case of 1988, the Court considered the constitutionality of the North Carolina Charitable Solicitations Act. This law had been passed after the state learned that the five largest fundraising firms were retaining more than 80% of the donations that they collected. The law banned such companies from charging "unreasonable" or "excessive" fees. It also required them to disclose the charity's fundraising costs to a prospective donor prior to soliciting any contribution. Furthermore, fundraising companies would need to obtain a license from the state.

After the losses that Schaumburg and Maryland had both suffered, North Carolina really should have known better than to put any limit on fundraising fees. This section of the law was, predictably, struck down by a 7-2 vote. But then the Court went further: the disclosure requirement was invalid as well. Forcing someone to speak about an unpleasant topic—like how much "charitable" money was lining his pockets—was just as bad as preventing him from speaking at all.

As an additional win for the telemarketers, the licensing requirement for professional fundraisers was rejected too. By a vote of 6-3, the Court deemed it to be a "prior restraint" on a charity's freedom of speech. The prior restraint rule is an important part of First Amendment jurisprudence, and it can be summed up in one sentence: no one should have to get the government's permission before saying something. But Rehnquist (who was by now the Chief Justice) was exasperated once more, and again wrote a dissenting opinion. He observed that North Carolina certainly requires an attorney to be licensed before he or she can argue on a client's behalf. So why can't the state also require a fundraising firm to get a license? Nonetheless, Rehnquist was on the losing side, and *Riley* was (and still is) the law of the land.

Thanks to this line of decisions, and especially the *Riley* case, states have limited options available for policing charitable telemarketing. They cannot force solicitors to be licensed, but can still require them to file registration forms and financial disclosure statements. If a donor wants to investigate where his money is going, he must ask the attorney general's office for a copy of these records. Today it is sometimes possible to find this data on the web, but in 1988 it was somewhat less convenient. You would need to file a request by mail and pay a fee for postage and copying expenses. By the time the information arrived, your opportunity to make a generous gift to the Western Appalachian Paramedics Society would be gone until its next telephone fundraising drive two months later.

The *Riley* opinion helped usher in the Golden Age of Tele-Panhandling. And for those who didn't appreciate the frequent phone calls, and who wanted to retaliate, it also ushered in the Golden Age of Being a Smart Ass. Here's an example of how the recipient of a fundraising call could make a solicitor feel uncomfortable:

> Homeowner (while chewing dinner): "Mmmmph.... Hello."
> Caller: "Good evening, sir, this is Keith at the State Police Association."
> Homeowner (nervously): "The state police? What's this about?"
> Caller: "Last year, Trooper J. L. Johnson was killed while conducting a traffic stop on Highway 62. Our organization..."
> Homeowner (interrupting): "I swear I had nothing to do with it! And I'm not saying anything else without my attorney present."
> Caller: "Umm... OK, sir, have a good day."

If the kids were out of the room, you could try this one:

> Homeowner: "Hello."
> Caller: "Hi, Mrs. Loomis? This is Melissa from the Special Olympics, how are you?"
> Homeowner: "Thanks for calling, Melissa, but my husband and I aren't going to compete this year. Last time we were sore for weeks, and now we're four years older so I doubt we'll win another medal."
> Caller (incredulously): "You were in the Special Olympics, ma'am?"
> Homeowner: "Oh, I thought you said the *Sexual* Olympics. What's the Special Olympics? Is that similar to the X-Rated Games, or is it more like a naked horseshoes tournament?"
> Caller (muttering to herself): "I never should have dropped out of nursing school and taken this horrible job."

The good times continued with the passage of the TCPA in 1991. Thanks to the FCC's loophole, non-profit groups (and their for-profit fundraisers) were largely exempted from the law. And with other types of telemarketers now having to contend with the TCPA's ban on sales robocalls to homes, there was less noise drowning out the pleas for contributions.

Of course, the TCPA did add one new restriction on charitable groups: they could not make robocalls to cell phones without prior permission. Few groups expressed any concern about this when Congress was writing the legislation. At the time, a mobile phone was not the convenient personal accessory that it is today. Only well-to-do people owned one, since it was expensive to buy and calls could cost fifty cents a minute or more. Plus it required a valet to carry it, because it weighed as much as a brick and sported an antenna long enough to knock cobwebs down from the ceiling of a cathedral. Obviously, most users of cellular phones were engaged in important business such as launching hostile corporate takeovers or negotiating billion-dollar credit swaps. They needed a phone with them at every moment because thousands of people's livelihoods depended on their whims.

There was no sensible rationale for a charity to blast out unsolicited robocalls to the A-list crowd who possessed mobile phones. Anyone who did so would certainly be regarded as the most insolent of trespassers. Could you imagine wasting a wealthy mogul's time with a pathetic prerecorded message asking for a laughable $20 contribution to your organization? The proper way to obtain a donation from a cell phone owner in 1991 was to get in touch with his agent, host a black-tie gala in his honor, and then name a school or hospital building after him. And here's a tip from 2019: have an alternate building name in mind for when the donor later says something offensive or is accused of sexual harassment. Goodbye, "Harvey Weinstein Cafeteria." Hello, "Main Dining Hall."

Today, obviously, many people simply can't be reached without calling their cell phones, and yet organizations can risk ruinous liability if they don't filter these numbers out of their dialing lists. But even as TCPA litigation has increased, and more charities have become reliant on predictive dialers and robocalls, it is still relatively rare for fundraising calls to trigger a lawsuit. Part of the reason is that most folks have some moral reluctance to go after the assets of a non-profit group. No one wants to bankrupt an organization that is working on a vaccine for athlete's foot, or that provides free skateboarding lessons to Korean War veterans.

The bigger reason, however, is that non-profits have such a lucrative racket going on with landlines that they rarely have any desire to dial mobile numbers. Aside from the older (and presumably more generous) demographics of landline households, it's easier to get a favorable response from a donor when he or she is comfortable at home. If you call and beg a stranger for money when he's driving in rush hour traffic, or while he's busy dumping beer on a visiting player from the stands at a Mets game, you aren't going to get a donation pledge. Instead, you'll probably be discourteously instructed to perform an unnecessary proctological procedure on yourself. So, most charity fundraisers make a solid effort to avoid calling cell numbers without permission. And many of them have a very good lawyer on their side, helping ensure that they don't do anything that will violate the TCPA and cost them millions of dollars. That lawyer's name is Errol Copilevitz.

In the 1970s and 1980s, it was fashionable for crusading prosecutors to harass adult entertainment establishments by accusing them of violating zoning ordinances and obscenity laws. Errol Copilevitz defended these businesses when many other attorneys would not, and in the process he became an expert on First Amendment law. He also cultivated a clientele in the traveling carnival industry. If your circus hippo happened to escape its cage and terrorize the public, Copilevitz was the guy who could smooth things over with the authorities. (This isn't a hypothetical; he actually once handled a case like that.) Because these carnivals often claimed (with varying degrees of accuracy) to be donating their proceeds to charities, he developed close ties to the non-profit fundraising sector. And when the *Riley* case was heard by the Supreme Court, it was Errol Copilevitz who stood before the justices and delivered the winning argument.

Today, the Kansas City law firm Copilevitz, Lam & Raney (formerly Copilevitz & Canter) is the number one defender of professional panhandlers in the United States. A 2013 investigation by the *Tampa Bay Times* and the Center for Investigative Reporting designated fifty charities as the worst in the nation based on the smallest percentages of money that went toward helping anyone in need. Copilevitz's firm represented thirty-seven of them. When confronted with that statistic, Copilevitz pointed out that he also works with some of the best charities. It's his job to zealously advocate for his clients, not to distinguish which ones are good and which ones aren't. That task can be handled by the *Tampa Bay Times*.

Copilevitz's services are in demand now more than ever, because some new legal and practical challenges have emerged for non-profit fundraisers in this century. After the 9/11 attacks in 2001, there were concerns that fake charities would attempt to exploit the tragedy. Congress responded by enacting the Crimes Against Charitable Americans Act (CACAA). To avoid having people pronounce it as "ca-ca," legislators welded it onto the USA PATRIOT Act which was quickly passed and signed by President George W. Bush. This law ordered the FTC to expand its definition of telemarketing to include charitable solicitations. The Telemarketing Sales Rule (TSR), which bans abusive and deceptive practices, would now apply to fundraising calls just as it would for sales calls.

In its haste to pass this law, Congress forgot one detail: the FTC has never been granted jurisdiction over charities, churches, or F.O.P. lodges. The "T" in its name stands for "trade," not "tithing." Faced with this quandary, the FTC had to be careful in how it wrote its expanded telemarketing regulations. Non-profit groups themselves would still not be covered by the TSR, but their third-party fundraisers would be. As a practical matter, this is not a huge limitation on the rule. Most charities can't tell the difference between a predictive dialer and a paper shredder, so they must use outside firms to operate their telephone campaigns. This means that the TSR does indeed apply to the vast majority of fundraising calls.

But the bigger issue for tele-panhandlers is the competition that they now face from others who seek our attention. As phone calls, texts, and emails have increased dramatically over the past ten to fifteen years, the likelihood of any one call being successful has diminished. It's rarely cost effective to use live solicitors anymore, at least for the initial contact with a potential donor. Yet, a simple prerecorded message that begs for money will almost certainly be ignored. For this reason, many fundraisers today have settled on a hybrid solution: the soundboard.

A soundboard device lets you play snippets of someone else's voice, or other sound effects, by pushing buttons on a computer. The first soundboards were intended primarily for prank phone calls by "morning zoo" radio programs. The radio hosts would pretend to be Hollywood stars and politicians, and would play a series of incongruous celebrity sound bites during a call. They would then broadcast the reaction of a dry cleaner who believes Sylvester Stallone is threatening to ruin her business over a torn shirt, or a male stripper who thinks Hillary Clinton is inviting him to her hotel room for a private performance. These stunts were a lot of fun, but it was easy to tell when you were being pranked. If Clint Eastwood says "make my day" four times while ordering a pizza, it's probably not really him on the line.

More sophisticated soundboards are available today. At their best, they can allow a person with a speech impediment to be gainfully employed as a telemarketer. He or she can direct the system to play scripted statements that have been recorded by a professional announcer who acts as an "avatar." If someone expresses interest in making a purchase or a donation, the worker can transfer the call to a more fluent employee. When everything is handled smoothly, the calls' recipients never realize that the first agent they heard was a recording.

This type of technology gained momentum in 2009 when the FTC toughened the TSR and banned most prerecorded fundraising calls. Soundboards were spared only because one telemarketer petitioned the FTC to exempt them. In its letter to the Commission, the company praised the soundboard as a valuable assistive device for disabled people. It was similar to the voice synthesizer used by the brilliant physicist Dr. Stephen Hawking to overcome one of the limitations of his illness. A soundboard can also mask an unpleasant accent or an annoying voice, thereby opening up new opportunities for Gilbert Gottfried and Roseanne Barr. Left unsaid was the potential for using the technology to move American jobs to overseas sweatshops, where they could be filled by agents with minimal English language skills.

The FTC responded favorably to the petition, agreeing that soundboards were not as problematic as recorded messages that couldn't be interrupted or challenged. The Commission decided to permit the devices, but only if they were used in the way that the telemarketer had portrayed. An agent must monitor the call at all times, and must be able to "continuously interact" with the other party to direct the conversation and respond to any concerns.

While this ruling opened up a hole in the TSR, the TCPA remained unchanged. It was still illegal to call cell phones with any type of prerecorded call without permission. Likewise, sales calls to residential landlines couldn't use recordings unless there was some kind of prior customer relationship. Charitable fundraising was the one profitable niche where soundboards were both legal and somewhat effective, and solicitors soon began taking full advantage of the FTC's exemption.

But recipients of these calls quickly discovered that they were nothing like having a conversation with Stephen Hawking. If you talked to him, you could ask virtually any science question and his electronic voice box would respond immediately with a thoughtful answer. He could probably have even told us what tau leptons taste like. Most people never get to try them, since they always seem to decay in a trillionth of a second each time someone makes a batch.

By contrast, a call from a soundboard wasn't much different from an ordinary robocall. You could ask a question, but the reply would be either a non sequitur or a disconnect. Clearly, there wasn't anyone listening attentively to these calls and controlling them as the FTC required. Maybe an employee was monitoring five or ten calls simultaneously. But more likely no one was paying attention at all, and the fundraising firms were using a speech recognition system to discern which calls should be transferred to a live agent. This software understood phrases like "I want to contribute," and "Please help yourself to my daughter's college fund." Other commonly heard expressions, such as "Quit calling me, you @&#% stupid robot," were evidently beyond its comprehension.

When the FTC learned that its regulations were being ignored, it summoned several soundboard users and manufacturers to its office in 2016. They explained to the Commission that it would be too expensive to hire enough agents to monitor each call individually. No one was ever going to do it. There had once been grandiose ideas about taking stutterers, mushmouths, and mimes out of the unemployment lines and putting them to work in call centers, where they would be given the sultry voice of Nina Blackwood or the clear diction of James Earl Jones. It was now obvious, however, that soundboard technology was just a way to make solicitations that were almost completely automated.

The Commission realized it had been played for a fool. It tried to revoke the TSR exemption that it had granted seven years earlier, but quickly faced legal action from the hastily-formed Soundboard Association. With Errol Copilevitz and his firm leading the charge, the group cited the usual First Amendment guidelines about content-based speech restrictions. It also assailed the FTC's rulemaking procedures with a technical argument that is far too boring to discuss here. (The author apologizes to any administrative law aficionados who were eager to learn about the distinction between an "interpretive rule" and a "final agency action.") The courts ruled in the Commission's favor, however, and in April 2019 the Supreme Court refused to hear the Soundboard Association's appeal.

Soundboards can still be used to call landlines legally in some scenarios, such as political polling. Charities can utilize them when making their own fundraising calls, though few organizations possess the know-how to do so. Also, third-party solicitors can still take advantage of soundboards when reaching out to previous donors or current members of a non-profit group. But what about all the other persistent fundraising calls that were being made to the public at large using this technology? A billion-dollar industry must now adapt to the loss of its favorite invention.

It's possible that fundraising firms will find some other innovation to replace soundboards. Or maybe they will go back to live solicitors, and compensate for the loss in efficiency by increasing their take of the proceeds from 85% all the way up to 98% or so. Another option is to simply ignore the rule and hope that they don't get caught for a while. This is feasible because the TSR doesn't include a meaningful private right of action like the TCPA does. Anyone who gets an illegal soundboard call on a landline has little recourse other than to submit a complaint to the FTC, where it will probably be lost in a pile with thousands of others.

You might find it hard to believe that any company would adopt this type of business model: violating the law routinely and deliberately with the expectation of not being held fully accountable. If so, you are in for a shock when you read the next chapter.

7. DEBT COLLECTORS: THE WORLD CHAMPIONS OF ROBOCALLING

Imagine if people could just borrow money and fritter it away without having the means or intention to ever pay it back. Actually, you don't have to imagine, because we have this already. It's called "Congress." But without the virtuous and respectable profession of the bill collector, America would have 300 million free-spending congressmen and congresswomen instead of 535. Our currency would quickly collapse, and we'd be reduced to a caveman-style barter system in which all purchases must be paid immediately with animal pelts or shiny rocks.

Collectors should be praised for keeping the economy afloat, but instead they are generally reviled. Part of the reason they are so unpopular is that they speak an entirely different language from the rest of the world. Linguistic differences are a known source of friction in human societies, as can be seen by the constant turmoil in the Canadian province of Quebec. There, French-speaking and English-speaking residents have fought bloody wars over whether there should be an accent mark over the first "e" in "Quebec." And if you ever meet someone from that region, don't get them started on whether the word "shampooing" is a verb or a noun.

With a little effort it is possible to crack the debt collection code. Here are translations of a few phrases that might be spoken by someone in the industry:

"We need to speak to you immediately about an important business matter."

<u>What a normal person hears</u>: An important business matter? Maybe a multinational company heard about those 4-H ribbons I won in high school, and it wants to hire me as its new CEO? Or perhaps I've been granted the exclusive right to ship fruit through the Suez Canal? Whichever it is, I need to call them back and wrap up this lucrative deal!

<u>What the collector means</u>: Your ex-husband forgot to return a satellite TV receiver when he was in college fifteen years ago. We want $600.

"Your account has been assigned to us for collection."

<u>What a normal person hears</u>: Oh crap, this must be about that Discover Card bill I couldn't pay when I lost my job during the recession. Now I have the combined forces of the Discover conglomerate and this debt collector on my tail. I'll have to join the merchant marines and spend a few years at sea until this blows over!

<u>What the collector means</u>: We bought a spreadsheet that shows you missed a Discover Card payment in 2008. Discover has written it off, and would probably give you another card if you asked, but if we can trick you into a new installment plan it will be pure profit for us. By the way, three other companies bought the same spreadsheet. You'll be hearing from them too.

"This is Lincoln Carnegie Franklin Federal Credit Corporation."

<u>What a normal person hears</u>: In 1853, the titans of American liberty and commerce founded a bank that provided the funds for westward expansion and the construction of the railroads. Today this historic firm needs my help, and it is my patriotic duty to pay them whatever they ask.

<u>What the collector means</u>: The judge told me I can't drive anymore. So, I sold my Corvette last month and used the cash to start this company in my garage with a couple of my stoner friends. Awesome name, huh? Pedro thought it up while he was smoking a huge-ass blunt.

"This call is for James Applespring. If you are not James Applespring, please hang up immediately. By staying on the line, you confirm you are James Applespring."

<u>What a normal person hears</u>: I can tell this is a debt collector, but they're trying to safeguard this guy's privacy by not revealing the purpose of the call to anyone but him. What a classy company.

<u>What the collector means</u>: James Applespring is a deadbeat, and a stubborn one at that. We're trying to embarrass him by robocalling everyone who lives within two miles of him and mentioning his name. He's a celebrity now!

Debt collectors don't just speak a different language than the rest of us; they also play by a different set of rules that is far more lenient. Let's consider a hypothetical. Suppose we have a friend named Hector whose ex-girlfriend never gave back the DVDs that she borrowed when they were dating last year. Hector starts calling her and messaging her to politely ask for the return of his property. After about three or four unsuccessful requests, he will be labeled a "stalker." If he persists, this hypothetical will end right here because Hector will be in prison.

Hector becomes despondent upon realizing that *The Complete Third Season of Frasier* will never be restored to its rightful place in his video library. He suffers a physical and mental breakdown and is hospitalized for three days. Unfortunately, his health insurance excludes coverage for any condition related to the *Cheers* franchise or its spin-offs. He is soon besieged by dozens upon dozens of robocalls concerning the medical bills that he will never be able to pay. He is harassed at home, at work, and while driving between home and work. Whenever Hector is watching seasons two and four of *Frasier* on his couch with a new female acquaintance, the romantic mood is spoiled by yet another call from a collector.

Legally, the never-ending calls to Hector do not constitute "stalking" or "telecommunications harassment" as they would if they were made by someone outside of the collections context. Hector can't get the police to take an interest in his case, and the courts won't issue a restraining order to protect him. His best option is to sue the abusive collectors for violating the Fair Debt Collection Practices Act (FDCPA).

At first glance, the FDCPA appears to provide some real benefits to consumers. It outlaws "false, deceptive, or misleading" representations by debt collectors. It prohibits conduct that will "harass, oppress, or abuse" anyone when seeking payment. It bars collection agencies from disclosing information about debtors to third parties. It requires collectors to provide validation of debts upon request, and to cease communication when instructed in writing. And there's much, much more.

However, the FDCPA's private right of action doesn't hold a candle to the one in the TCPA. For one thing, there is no strict liability. Collectors can avoid having to pay damages if they show that the violation was due to an unintentional "bona fide" mistake. The language of the law is also prone to varying interpretations, and so a slam-dunk case is rare. Do ten phone calls in a week constitute harassment? A plaintiff can probably find a court opinion that says yes, but the defendant will counter with one that reached the opposite conclusion. The outcome may depend on the exact wording of what the parties said to each other on the phone, so if there is no recording then the plaintiff might be out of luck. And he better not let the skimpy one-year statute of limitations run out!

In some cases the FDCPA doesn't even apply at all. The statute protects people only from third-party collection agencies and debt buyers, not from companies that are collecting money owed by their own customers. Suppose a bank—with a name that rhymes with "hell's cargo"—is trying to resolve your cousin's delinquent car loan. It might decide to robocall you repeatedly to see if she happens to be hiding out at your place. Or maybe a catalog merchandiser—whose name bears an unfortunate resemblance to that of a lewd act involving digital penetration—mistakenly accuses you of ordering an item and forgetting to pay. These are real world scenarios in which an FDCPA claim is going to fail from the outset, since these creditors' in-house collectors are immune from the law.

But the biggest problem with the FDCPA's private right of action is the damages part of the law. If you win your case, you are entitled to receive no more than $1,000. This amount has not been adjusted for inflation since the law was enacted in 1977, and it is not stackable. Even if the collector violates the law a hundred different times in a dozen different ways, you can still get only $1,000. Of course, laws always have exceptions, and one of them is if the plaintiff can prove actual damages that exceed the $1,000 limit. An emotionally fragile person like our friend Hector might be able to demand compensation for medical or counseling expenses arising from the harassment. But, unlike with the TCPA, the probability of a five- or six-figure individual payout in an FDCPA case is almost nil.

Even class actions don't carry much weight with the FDCPA. The damages for a class of plaintiffs who were wronged is limited to the *lesser* of either $500,000 or 1% of the collector's net worth. This makes it difficult to hold companies responsible when they commit widespread violations affecting hundreds of thousands of consumers. Lawyers will sometimes try to work around the limitation by filing separate class actions in each state where the defendant operates. This leads to uneven outcomes and (conveniently enough) more fees for all of the attorneys involved.

In extreme situations, the FTC will step in and enforce the FDCPA on its own. Here is one of the allegations from a Commission complaint in 2017:

> "In numerous instances, when Defendant has called persons to collect a debt, the persons have told Defendant that they are not the individuals who owe the debts that Defendant is attempting to collect. ... In numerous of these instances, despite being so informed, Defendant has continued to call these persons in an attempt to collect the debts."

Does this defendant resemble anyone you've read about recently? It was GC Services, the same company that had once fanatically pursued the supposed debtor "Darnell" like Captain Ahab hunting for a white whale. The FTC fined it $700,000 for its recklessness. This sounds like a suitable punishment, until you hear that GC Services is a large enterprise with annual revenues of well over $100 million. It could probably painlessly come up with the 700 grand just by grounding the corporate jet for a couple weeks, or by switching to one-ply toilet paper in the employee bathrooms.

The FTC once levied an even larger penalty for abusive telephone behavior: a $1.75 million fine against Allied Interstate in 2010. The Commission also permanently barred Allied from disobeying the FDCPA, which seemed like a totally unnecessary thing to do. The company was *already* barred from violating the FDCPA, because *it's the frigging law*. Allied should have taken the time to understand the statute's requirements *before* it decided to annoy the hell out of half the country.

However, even the FTC's harsh admonishment wasn't quite enough. In a later suit filed by Los Angeles County prosecutors,

Allied was ordered to pay another $9 million for subsequent transgressions of the FDCPA and other statutes. The district attorney noted that this was the eleventh law enforcement action against the company over a period of ten years. Unfortunately, the FDCPA doesn't authorize the government to revoke the corporate charter of a recalcitrant debt collector after the eleventh offense. If Allied Interstate were in China, its executives would have been brought before a firing squad long ago.

Despite all of the statute's shortcomings, and its apparent ineffectiveness, there are still around 10,000 FDCPA cases filed each year. That's because a winning plaintiff is entitled to a recovery of legal fees and costs in addition to the $1,000 of statutory damages. Debt collectors often complain to Congress, the FTC, and to random strangers on the subway about the supposed unfairness of this provision. They say that lawyers like to recruit clients who haven't suffered any discernible harm, and then use those clients to shake down innocent companies over minor technical errors. But there is another law that raises their dander more than any other: the TCPA.

The collections industry continually bitches and moans about the TCPA. They bitch, they moan, they pause to whine a little bit, and then they start the cycle over again with more bitching. And yet, they have been blessed with several extraordinary exemptions from this law. One of them was hinted at in Chapter 2, and now it's time to look at it in more detail.

In the late 1990s, collection agencies had a problem: the economy was fairly good and most people were paying their bills on time. Since the demand for their services was not increasing, they began taking a fresh look at how they could monetize older debts that had been written off as uncollectible. Many of these unpaid debts were not only outside of the statutes of limitations, which barred them from being enforced in courts, but were also past the seven-year limit that controlled whether they would show up on a credit report. In some cases they had been discharged by bankruptcy proceedings and were no longer valid. There was no financial reason for anyone to pay these debts now, but a small percentage of consumers could be harassed, cajoled, or shamed into doing so. The biggest difficulty was in tracking down the people who owed (or, stated more accurately, used to owe) this money.

A debtor who vanishes without leaving a forwarding address is known as a "skip," and the act of locating him or her is referred to as "skip tracing." When done correctly, skip tracing is both an art and a science. Skilled investigators will seek information from a target's relatives and associates, and will scour social media activity for clues. Databases of public records, such as LexisNexis' Accurint, can provide hints to where the target might be hiding out. Skip tracers know to treat these databases with skepticism, however, because they are riddled with inaccurate and outdated information.

Older debts pose special problems for skip tracers. For one thing, these are the tougher cases that have been worked by other investigators without success. Also, the documentation for them has often been lost. There may be only four key pieces of information in the file: a debtor's name, his or her Social Security number, an original creditor's name, and a monetary amount. This is all that remains after ownership of the obligation has passed from one company to another several times, traveling through multiple incompatible computer systems in the process. (The original creditor unloaded it for maybe 30% of face value a few months after it became delinquent, and is entirely indifferent as to whether it will ever be paid.) Even if the debtor is successfully located, it's all for naught if he asserts his rights under the FDCPA and demands to see proof that he owes the money. The chance of unearthing a signed contract is quite slim indeed.

For these reasons, a debt that is beyond its statute of limitations is almost completely devoid of value. Antiquated debts are worth pursuing only when they can be bundled in a batch with thousands of others and processed together. This requires automation, and lots of it. Skip tracing must be replaced by a technique that investigators derisively call "skip guessing." The entire set of debts is checked with Accurint or a similar product, and each record is loosely matched to several possible addresses and phone numbers. Neighbors and likely relatives are sometimes added to the data as well. Finally, each of these leads is followed up with another automated process. Maybe letters are printed and mailed, or maybe the phone numbers are loaded into a predictive dialer and called by collections specialists. But in most cases, the likelihood of recovering a payment is too low to justify even the modest expenditures required for those efforts. This is where robocalls—a plentiful and virtually free resource—have some appeal.

Debt collection robocalls increased as agencies rediscovered old debts and began working them using this automated scattershot approach. Then the job market tanked in 2002, dumping a new surge of delinquent bills into the collections pipeline. This led to an even higher volume of unsolicited and largely unproductive calls. Within a few years, many consumers were looking for an effective recourse against this incessant nuisance.

One such consumer was James Watson. Ever since the first rude interruption by Alexander Graham Bell in 1876, people named "Watson" have faced more than their share of unwanted phone calls. James was no exception. Soon after moving into a new home in Florida in August 2005, he realized why the previous owner had left: the house was possessed by an evil spirit. That was the only explanation for why his phone would receive the same anonymous prerecorded message every single day:

> "Please call 1-877-803-8009. This message is not a solicitation call. It is in regards to a important business matter that needs your immediate attention. ..."

The cheerless voice then rambled for another minute as it recited its business hours in painful detail. This mysterious caller didn't even have a name, and yet it was open on Sundays.

Watson undertook a heroic effort to stop these calls. He dialed the toll-free number in the message on several occasions, and spoke to customer service representatives in New Delhi, Montreal, and Mumbai. He filed a complaint with the sheriff's office. He paid for a blocking feature offered by his phone company, which was promptly defeated by Caller ID spoofing. He did everything but summon a priest to hold an exorcism. His diocese must have had too long of a waiting list for that.

The problem was not resolved until December of that year, after Watson had received roughly two hundred robocalls and had devoted fifty-three hours of his time to the matter. The calls had clearly disregarded the FDCPA, and had also violated state tort law regarding invasion of privacy, intrusion upon seclusion, and being an insufferable jerk. Watson's lawyers tracked down the party that was responsible for them: a Pennsylvania collection agency called NCO. He filed suit against both NCO and its client Capital One, which owned the alleged debt, and he tacked on a TCPA allegation for placing robocalls to a residential landline without consent. If Watson prevailed on the TCPA claim, he would be entitled to a minimum of $100,000 in damages.

In its defense, NCO argued that the TCPA was never intended to apply to debt collectors. This was true up to a point. When members of Congress spoke in favor of the new law in 1991, they noted that many businesses used prerecorded calls for contact with their established clientele. In some cases, these calls were an efficient way to remind customers about payments that were past due. Although the TCPA contained a general ban on most robocalls to home landline phones, Congress didn't want valuable communications such as payment notices to be outlawed. So, the law authorized the FCC to exempt:

> "... such classes or categories of calls ... as the Commission determines will not adversely affect the privacy rights that this section is intended to protect; and do not include the transmission of any unsolicited advertisement;"

This is a little confusing, but the commissioners put on their thinking caps and crafted a reasonable rule. Robocalls that are part of an "established business relationship" would be OK because they do not hurt anyone's privacy. The FCC observed that "all debt collection circumstances involve a prior or existing business relationship," and so this exemption was sufficient to protect collectors.

Unfortunately for the defendants, they had no established business relationship with James Watson. He was not a Capital One customer and, according to his complaint, he owed NCO precisely zero dollars and zero cents. So this exemption would not help them, but there was another one that was much broader. The FCC had also decided to permit *all* residential robocalls that do not "include or introduce an advertisement or constitute telemarketing." This fit the circumstances perfectly, because NCO's prerecorded calls didn't include any advertisements. In fact, they contained no information of any value whatsoever. A telemarketing message would have been an improvement.

If you weren't confused a couple of paragraphs ago, you should be by now. Why did the FCC put this colossal hole in the TCPA? Wasn't the Commission only allowed to exempt calls that don't conflict with people's privacy rights? And what was the point of the "established business relationship" rule if obscure companies—with initials instead of names—were permitted to robocall everyone anyway? You won't find any answers here, nor in the FCC's official record of its rulemaking proceedings. It's possible that the Commission simply misread the statute, but nearly thirty years later it has still not fixed the error.

Judge Legrome Davis was faced with a dilemma. The Supreme Court had ruled, in the landmark *Chevron* case of 1984, that judges should defer to federal agencies' interpretation of the law. This would require him to respect the FCC's exemption and throw out Watson's TCPA claim against NCO and Capital One. However, this doctrine of "*Chevron* deference" only goes so far. When an agency's rules conflict with a law that Congress has passed, it is the law that should prevail. That put the FCC's broad exemption on shaky ground, because the Commission had skipped a required step in the rulemaking process. It hadn't adequately considered which calls would "adversely affect the privacy rights" of consumers.

Additionally, the Commission had started from a dubious premise: "all debt collection circumstances involve a prior or existing business relationship." This might not have been an unreasonable belief in 1992. No one predicted that collectors would someday pluck phone numbers from an unreliable database and then audaciously robocall them hundreds of times on the remote chance that a long-lost debtor would answer. But that was the new reality, and Davis' ruling addressed it quite well:

> "[T]he FCC made [the exemption] under the assumption that debt collection calls would be made only to debtors (i.e. those with an established business relationship). Because the facts of this case belie that assumption, the FCC's pronouncement does not address the privacy rights implicated here. The fact is, by virtue of staying out of debt, a non-debtor has vastly greater privacy rights than someone who has fallen into debt. While the

FCC has declared that a debtor's privacy rights are not adversely affected when he receives debt collection calls, the Court is convinced that a non-debtor's rights are in fact violated when he is subjected to repeated annoying and abusive debt collection calls that he remains powerless to stop."

The defendants' motion to dismiss was denied, and they were compelled to negotiate a settlement on unfavorable terms. Although we don't know how much Watson was paid, it's a safe bet that his next car included the luxury package with a sunroof and leather seats. He probably also got a grin on his face every time he heard one of those Capital One commercials that asked "What's in your wallet?" He knew exactly what was in his wallet: a big pile of Capital One's (and NCO's) money.

However, this was not the last word on the FCC's loophole. Because Watson's case was decided at the district court level, and never affirmed by an appellate court, the ruling was not binding upon anyone else. In fact, most courts chose to disregard Judge Davis' opinion.

As an example, consider the sad episode that unfolded in Buffalo, New York in 2009. A collection agency wanted to talk to Hazel Meyers about an unpaid bill, but it didn't know her phone number. So, it had one of its employees repeatedly call an unrelated family, the Santinos, and ask to speak to Hazel. Maybe if they did this often enough, Mr. and Mrs. Santino would eventually hire an investigator with their own money to track Hazel down for them. Mrs. Santino instead argued with the collector, who called her a "liar" when she told him he had reached the wrong number. The company then began using an automated dialer and prerecorded phone messages to harass the family on a daily basis.

The collection agency in this case was a familiar one: NCO. (Illegal robocalling has a very high rate of recidivism.) The Santinos sued NCO and cited Watson's case as a precedent. Although the judge agreed with them that "*Watson* might be seen as persuasive on a common sense level," he believed the Supreme Court's *Chevron* guidelines required him to uphold the FCC's exemption. He noted that the Commission had been given another chance to address the issue in 2008, post-*Watson*, but had perfunctorily reaffirmed its previous regulations. With this ruling, the TCPA portion of the

Santinos' lawsuit was dismissed. They were left with only a wimpy FDCPA claim, but at least their lawyers were still looking at a decent payday.

Judges have reached this same conclusion in virtually all subsequent cases involving misdirected debt collection calls to landline phones. They honor the FCC's loophole, even though it is difficult to explain or justify. This has been part of a larger pattern of treating the Commission's guidance with not just deference, but outright reverence. Until recently, courts have almost uniformly abided by the FCC's TCPA decrees.

You may have spotted another legal problem with NCO's anonymous robocalls in the *Watson* case. The TCPA's technical and procedural standards require companies to identify themselves by their true names at the start of all automated phone messages. Those who fail to do so can be fined. This has been a source of consternation for collectors, because the FDCPA contains a conflicting mandate that is intended to protect a debtor's privacy. Agents are not supposed to blurt out their employers' identities until they have verified they are talking to the right person. No prerecorded message can conform to both sets of rules, so carelessly robocalling the wrong number is guaranteed to break either one law or the other.

The obvious solution is for collection agencies to stop using prerecorded calls unless they are reasonably sure that they are dialing the correct phone number. This kind of seems like a good idea anyway, doesn't it? It would force them to hire more workers, however, so it's off the table. Instead, the Commission has assured collectors that it will not punish them for omitting the required identification.

When it comes to its treatment of debt collectors, the FCC has in many ways been like a cool, easygoing dad. "Go ahead and have your friends over for a robocalling party while Mom and I are out of town! We're getting new carpet next month, so it's OK if someone pukes." But up until now, we've mainly been talking about landline calls. Cell phones are like the room that the otherwise permissive dad forbids you to enter without adult supervision. This is where he keeps his golf clubs, his vinyl albums, and the bottle of twenty-year-old Scotch that he plans to celebrate with when the mortgage is paid off. If your guests drink Dad's whisky, use his putter to unclog the toilet, and play his *Christmas with Glen Campbell* record backwards to listen for demonic messages, you know there will be serious consequences later.

In the original version of the TCPA, Congress left no wiggle room in the ban on autodialed and prerecorded calls to wireless phones, emergency lines, and hospital rooms. These types of calls could be made only "for emergency purposes or ... with the prior express consent of the called party." End of discussion. But it amended this part of the law the following year, and the FCC was now authorized to exempt calls to cell phones that don't result in a charge to the recipient. (It was required to consider consumers' privacy rights when making any exemption, but we already know how that goes.) At the time, not many people had cell phones, and those who did usually had to pay by the minute. This new provision of the law was intended mainly to let wireless providers deliver automated billing and service messages to their own customers without charging them. However, when unlimited usage phone plans began to dominate the market many years later, it also offered debt collectors and some other types of businesses an excuse to petition the FCC for a new loophole.

These business groups wanted the Commission to eviscerate the cell phone robocall ban, just as it had done with the residential robocall rule. They asked for an exemption for "informational" calls, which they conveniently defined to include virtually any kind of communication from a debt collector. They requested an exemption for calls that were made to the wrong party by mistake. They also begged, pleaded, and positively groveled before the commissioners, asking them to reconsider their 2003 ruling in which they classified predictive dialers as automatic dialing systems. But it was like talking to a brick wall, except that they could have talked to a wall for free without hiring lobbyists. The FCC may have realized what a blunder it had made with its lenient regulations for landline robocalls, and was determined not to repeat the mistake with cell phones.

Having no luck with the FCC, debt collectors tried to persuade courts to see things their way. They would have plenty of chances to do so, since TCPA lawsuits against them accelerated shortly after the Wall Street meltdown of 2008. This was due to a combination of factors, with the economic upheaval being the least of them. More significant was the collision between two trends. Collectors were depending more heavily on robocalls and automated dialers at precisely the same time that consumers were abandoning their landline phones and going wireless-only. And yet, few of the players in the business anticipated the costly deluge of litigation that was barreling toward them.

By this time, some companies known as "bottom feeders" were focusing exclusively on buying up expired debts that no one else would touch. Their goal was not just to demand payments on these worthless obligations; it was to lure unsophisticated consumers into confusing new timed payment plans that would restart the statutes of limitations. Many of these plans would then go into default, triggering onerous fees and penalties and ensuring another round of business for the collectors. Robocalls were an essential part of this business model, and were used both for locating and harassing those who had unpaid bills in their distant past. Since these calls cost only a fraction of a cent, why not make as many as possible? What could go wrong?

As we know, much went wrong. Ignorance of the law was rampant in the industry. Some collectors couldn't have spelled TCPA even if you gave them the first three letters. Others thought they were calling only landline phone numbers, but forgot to check the portability database to find out which of those numbers had been converted to cellular service. And many of the bottom feeders knew they weren't compliant, but didn't care. Meanwhile, despite all of the FCC's blustering about predictive dialers and what-not, its enforcement bureau was looking the other way as collectors openly defied the Commission's strict regulations.

These companies could afford to be indifferent about the TCPA for a while, because few consumers had ever heard of the statute. That was about to change, as websites such as Debtorboards and BudHibbs.com encouraged individuals to exchange tips about suing abusive debt collectors. And when robocalling victims turned to the internet for help with deciphering the strange phone numbers that kept appearing on their Caller ID displays, they would often be directed to advertisements for law firms. "Has XYZ Receivables called your cell phone? You may be entitled to up to $1,500 per call!" Accountability was on its way, but not from the government. It would be private citizens waging the fight.

When lackadaisical collection agencies were finally made to answer for their misdeeds, many of them were indignant. Their reactions seemed to have been learned from *Seinfeld*'s George Costanza, who defended himself defiantly when his boss learned about his indelicate dalliance atop a desk with the office cleaning lady. "All I did was repeatedly harass thousands of people and their family members, employers, and neighbors. I had no idea that sort of thing was frowned upon!" This type of non-apology was difficult to accept the first time it was heard, and even harder to believe after the same companies were sued five times, ten times, or more without repudiating their illegal practices.

The cell phone robocall lawsuits led to inconsistent results at first. Judges often found the language of the TCPA to be confusing, and the FCC's regulations added another layer of complexity on top. In addition, the Supreme Court didn't issue its *Mims* ruling until 2012, so many of the earlier cases were filed in state courts under varying sets of rules. When an attorney wanted to argue for a specific interpretation of the law, there was rarely a previous court decision that could be cited as authority either for or against that position. That allowed the parties to put forth some questionable lines of reasoning in the hope that judges who were unfamiliar with the statute could be fooled.

For example, some creditors believed that unsolicited robocalls to cellular phones should be legal unless consumers were billed for them. The FCC had already rejected this position, observing that the cost of the wireless airtime was only part of the rationale for the TCPA's restrictions. The calls could also pose safety concerns if they clogged cellular networks or distracted people while they were driving. Plus, they were universally agreed to be really, really annoying. But collectors countered by pointing to this language from the statute:

> "It shall be unlawful for any person within the United States to make [an automated call] ... to any telephone number assigned to a paging service, cellular telephone service, specialized mobile radio service, or other radio common carrier service, or any service for which the called party is charged for the call;"

The last phrase of this paragraph extends the TCPA's rules against robocalls to toll-free "1-800" lines in which businesses are charged for incoming long distance calls. It also protects consumers who have voice-over-IP phones that require them to pay for usage by the minute. Astute readers will note that the "charged for the call" clause is preceded by an "or." Despite the obvious meaning of this conjunction, some defendants insisted that the clause was intended to limit, rather than expand, the scope of the law. This was a difficult textual argument to make, bordering upon the preposterous, but it still occasionally had an effect. Even though it was highly unlikely to persuade a judge, it could trigger enough uncertainty to convince the plaintiff to take a lowball settlement offer.

Virtually every word in the law could be the focus of some kind of debate. Consider the word "make." Most other types of defendants would quickly concede that they "made" all the calls that are listed in their dialing records, but debt collectors do not give up so easily. They argued that "make" actually meant "consummate." If a call wasn't answered, and nobody heard the brilliantly scripted message that the collector had recorded, then it shouldn't count toward damages under the TCPA. It was just like the proverbial tree falling in the forest with no one around to Instagram it.

But the industry's optimism about this defense was once again misplaced, as courts consistently ruled that a call is "made" the moment it is dialed. It doesn't matter if the plaintiff never answered the call, or if he never even heard the ring, or if his phone had fallen into a swimming pool the previous day and was still drying out in a pile of rice. In one case from Texas, a woman complained that a collection agency had made 98 wrong number robocalls to her cell phone over the course of six months during 2008. She had only answered about four of the calls. A jury awarded her triple damages for each call that was dialed, for a total of $147,000, and the verdict was upheld on appeal. It was another painful lesson that the noisome tactics that had been used with landlines were no longer going to be tolerated in a world full of mobile devices.

There was still one solid legal and ethical defense that was available in some cases: a person can't complain about a robocall if he agreed to receive it. Under the TCPA, a call to a cell phone is legal if made "with the prior express consent of the called party." In early 2008, the FCC clarified the meaning of this phrase. It decreed that a consumer who offers up his phone number as part of a credit transaction is also consenting to receive automated collection calls at that number. In this way, implied consent is just as effective as the express consent that was mentioned in the law. The Commission had once again played fast and loose with the words of the statute, but this time the result was not terribly unreasonable.

It wasn't a total win for the industry, however, because the FCC put three big restrictions on how this would work. First, the consent does not extend to any other cell phone numbers belonging to the same person, such as numbers found during skip tracing. Second, the creditor has the burden of proof to show that consent was given. This was a problem for all of the bottom feeders who were chasing ten-year-old debts without adequate documentation. And third, although the FCC didn't pontificate on this topic until several years later, it was generally understood that the consumer could revoke his or her consent at any time. The courts would soon confirm this last assumption.

For an example of the complexities of this defense, consider what happened in 2009 when a Florida man became ill and went to a hospital emergency room. He was too sick to complete the paperwork, so his wife signed a form on his behalf and listed his cell number as a point of contact. The man then declined to pay his radiologist bill of $49.03. Consequently, he received several unwelcome automated phone calls from a collection agency, and retaliated by filing a class action TCPA lawsuit.

There is a seemingly endless stream of issues raised by this case. Was the wife authorized to give out the husband's cell number? When she wrote the number on a standard health records release form, was she giving express consent for collections calls or only implied consent? Did the hospital have permission to pass the phone number along to the radiologist, who was working for a separate company? Does the FCC's 2008 ruling apply to medical treatment settings like this, or only to credit applications? Is the FCC's ruling even valid anyway, or does it fail the *Chevron* deference test? And is it too late for one of us to send the doctor a check for $49.03 so that we don't have to hurt our brains thinking about all this?

These were all close questions that could have gone either way, and the outcome reflects that. At the district court level, the judge ruled for the plaintiff. However, the case was appealed to the 11th Circuit, which reached the opposite conclusions on nearly every point of law. If the district judge had opined that puppy dogs are cute, the appellate court would probably have found an ugly one just so it could prove him wrong. The suit was thrown out, and summary judgment was issued for the defendant. Ultimately, it was the fine print on the hospital's release form that saved the collection agency from a multimillion-dollar mess.

Although most robocallers are a pustule on the tonsils of society, the Case of the Unpaid X-Ray Bill gives us a different perspective. Sometimes the people who receive the calls can be a little pustule-like themselves. In the next chapter we'll see how they can use the TCPA in nefarious ways that Senator Hollings could not have imagined.

8. TURNING ROBOCALLS (AND FAXES) INTO RICHES

Gene Kalsky is an American success story. In 1994, while still in his thirties, he founded Gen-Kal Pipe & Steel. If you are looking for any kind of pipe, tubing, or other hollow cylindrical conveyance, chances are good that this company will have what you need. Somehow, Gen-Kal still isn't a household name, but its owner's hard work and entrepreneurial spirit have paid off for him and his employees. Kalsky now lives in a beautiful oceanfront home valued at more than $2 million.

Many of Gen-Kal's customers, typically plumbing suppliers or other industrial wholesalers, have never quite figured out the internet. They prefer to do business by fax. There is something about the long transmission times, wasted paper and ink, and frequent equipment breakdowns that gives them a warm and comforting feeling. Who needs the instant gratification of an email or a text message when you can fall back on the familiarity of the fax machine?

Gen-Kal promoted its special deals with fax advertising for many years. Knowing that it's unethical to send unsolicited advertisements by fax, it always asked each customer for permission to add it to Gen-Kal's marketing list. This was a smart thing to do, because TCPA litigation over junk faxes is still surprisingly common. Some small businesses keep their fax machines around only so that they can sue anyone who sends them an unsolicited ad. Unfortunately, Gen-Kal wasn't aware of another development in the law.

As part of its 2003 crackdown on unwanted calls, the FCC had proposed tightening the TCPA's rules on fax marketing. Companies would need to obtain written permission before sending a fax advertisement. This would obviously be a big hassle in some circumstances, like when a potential customer phones a restaurant and asks it to fax a delivery menu to him. The restaurant would first need to fax a consent form to the customer and then wait for it to be signed and sent back. Most people won't want to navigate this burdensome procedure while hungry, and will instead eat the jar of expired Miracle Whip that they find in the back of the fridge.

Congress thought this was gross, so it passed a law to block these more stringent rules from going into effect. Under this law, sponsored by Senator Gordon Smith, marketers can adhere to a very loose definition of consent as long as they include an opt-out notice in each advertisement. The notice must give the recipient some simple instructions that can be followed to avoid similar marketing messages in the future. Everyone understood that this new law was intended to prevent nuisance TCPA lawsuits, at the cost of increasing the number of nuisance faxes. But as an attempt at legislative humor, Smith named it the "Junk Fax Prevention Act."

When the FCC issued its interpretation of the law, however, the joke was on Congress. (Haw haw, Gordon Smith.) The Commission enacted the so-called "Solicited Fax Rule," which required the opt-out message to be present in *every* commercial fax advertisement—even those that were sent with express consent. It also wrote several technical regulations about the format of the opt-out notice and the language that it needed to contain. And, unlike the more straightforward technical requirements for robocalls, these exacting rules were enforceable by consumers with the TCPA's strict liability private right of action. This was an almost perfect blueprint for abusive litigation. Do you want to make some easy money? Just set up a fax machine and give the number to several unsophisticated advertisers, then wait to see whose opt-out disclaimer doesn't meet all of the FCC's nitpicking requirements.

In December 2015, Gene Kalsky's holiday celebrations at his home in New Jersey were marred by the delivery of a court summons. One of Gen-Kal's long-time customers was suing because the company had faxed it an ad that didn't fully comply with the FCC's Solicited Fax Rule. The advertisement had neglected to inform the customer that Gen-Kal must stop sending faxes within thirty days of receiving an opt-out request. This omission entitled the plaintiff to an award of $500.

Legally speaking, Gen-Kal Pipe & Steel Corporation and Gene Kalsky are two separate people. If, say, Gen-Kal were to inadvertently sell someone a pipe containing a venomous snake, Gene wouldn't be personally liable for any injuries that occur. (There are exceptions, of course, like if he brought his pet cobra to the warehouse and carelessly let it mingle with the merchandise.) But the plaintiff in the fax case had decided to sue both the company and its owner using a maneuver called "piercing the corporate veil." This tactic is typically used against very small businesses whose property is intermingled with that of their owners. It was a tough argument to make against Gen-Kal, but if it worked then Kalsky's personal assets would be available to satisfy any judgment. If the company refused to pay the $500, then maybe the plaintiff could stop by Kalsky's house and help itself to his garden gnomes and his propane grill.

The customer was located in Russellville, Arkansas, and had opted to sue in its local county court. This was an inconvenient venue for Kalsky, who needed to travel 1,300 miles to defend himself. It wasn't worth the trip even with possible triple damages of $1,500 on the line. He could have hired a lawyer in Arkansas to appear on his behalf, but again that seemed like a waste of money for such a trivial and—quite frankly—stupid matter. Kalsky was no attorney, but he decided that it was best to handle this nuisance on his own.

He typed a one-page letter of protest, and sent it to both the customer's attorney and the court. "We take the fax laws seriously in my office," he wrote in his defense. He explained that Gen-Kal had obtained the plaintiff's permission for the faxes via a phone conversation more than ten years earlier, and there had been no requests for the advertisements to stop. Kalsky suggested that the plaintiff pay him $1,000 for wasting his time with the "ridiculous" complaint. He concluded with a plea to the judge: "I respectfully request that this claim against me be dismissed."

This letter was concise, well-written, and persuasive. It was also a terrible, life-altering mistake. Before sending this response, Kalsky had arguably done nothing as an individual that would put him within the court's jurisdiction. He hadn't sold pipes to any plumbers in Pope County, Arkansas, nor had he sent any faxes there. It was his company that did those things. But by asking for dismissal in the way that he did, he was acknowledging that the court had the right to treat him personally as a defendant. Kalsky had just forfeited one of his best defenses.

The judge did not dismiss the suit as requested in the letter, but he did note that the allegations were disputed. The plaintiff would need to proceed with discovery, which meant interrogatories, subpoenas, and the like. Several times over the ensuing months, certified letters would arrive in New Jersey. Actually, they would arrive as pairs of identical letters: one for the Gen-Kal corporation and one for Kalsky himself. Kalsky signed for the letters but did not respond to them. He also steadfastly declined to seek legal advice. A lawyer would probably tell him to offer a settlement, and in his view that would be giving in to extortion.

One of the letters from Arkansas should have come with flashing red lights and an alarm bell. It was a motion to certify the suit as a class action. This letter was duly ignored like the others, and so the court appointed the plaintiff to represent everyone in the United States who had received a deficient fax from Gen-Kal in the preceding four years. Since Kalsky's company was not cooperating with discovery, its list of fax contacts was unavailable and there was no easy way to know who was part of this class. A notice to the potential victims was published in the December 2016 edition of *Supply House Times*, a magazine that caters to wholesale distributors of plumbing, HVAC, and industrial equipment. Thankfully it wasn't the popular summer swimsuit issue, so the embarrassment was minimized.

Kalsky also received a document entitled "Requests for Admission." It listed several allegations and asked him to either admit or deny them. By this time the busy entrepreneur was growing weary of the one-way correspondence. Where was *his* opt-out notice? He certainly had no interest in playing a silly "truth or dare" type of game like the one presented by the Requests for Admission. But when he blew off this letter, the judge deemed all of the accusations to be admitted. They included an unsupported claim that he and his company had sent at least 25,000 illegal faxes.

Finally the plaintiff filed a motion for summary judgment. Hearing no objection, or any other sign of the defendants' interest in the proceedings, the court granted the motion. Judgment was rendered against Kalsky and his beloved small business, jointly and severally, in the amount of $500. That is, $500 for *each* fax that he had inadvertently admitted to sending, for a total of $12,500,000. Gen-Kal's assets, which were valued at a few hundred thousand dollars, were frozen and it had no choice but to file for bankruptcy protection. The Cape May County sheriff also announced a foreclosure auction at which Kalsky's oceanfront residence would be sold to pay the debt.

Kalsky now realized that he needed to overcome his phobia of lawyers. It would take quite a few of them to clean up the mess he had created. He hired attorneys in Arkansas to try to get the judgment set aside, even though all of the deadlines for doing so had passed. Meanwhile, another law firm handled Gen-Kal's bankruptcy. There were also lawyers in Washington, D.C., asking the FCC to issue a retroactive waiver of the Solicited Fax Rule just for this case. And Kalsky's personal attorneys were arguing in the local courts in New Jersey, trying to prevent the seizure of his home.

As of this writing, it is only the last of these lawyers who are having any impact. The New Jersey courts noted that their judges are required to give full faith and credit to the actions of other states, but that they might decline to do so when a defendant has not been given due process of law. With that limitation in mind, the foreclosure auction has been postponed pending further proceedings. But don't be surprised if you see a brigade of Arkansas National Guard troops marching across the country to enforce their state's judges' orders.

As an ironic twist to this sad tale, the Solicited Fax Rule is no longer in force. Just two weeks after judgment was entered against Gen-Kal and Kalsky, the U.S. Court of Appeals for the District of Columbia Circuit ruled that the FCC had overstepped its bounds in requiring the opt-out notice on faxes that were sent with prior permission. Congress had authorized the Commission only to regulate unsolicited faxes. This 2-1 opinion, authored by a judge named Brett Kavanaugh, freed many fax advertisers from potential multimillion dollar losses. But since Kalsky had failed to raise this defense (or any other), it did him no good. Courts have a desire for finality and are not inclined to revisit closed cases just because the law has changed.

Gene Kalsky is now the official poster child of frivolous TCPA actions. Although he looks mighty good on the poster, he's not the only victim. Let's examine a questionable lawsuit that rocked the world of professional basketball a few years ago.

On October 13, 2012, David Emanuel attended a Los Angeles Lakers pre-season game at the Staples Center. His woman was with him and he couldn't have been happier. The Lakers encouraged fans to text them messages that would be displayed on the scoreboard for all of the spectators in the arena to see. Emanuel accepted the offer and penned these words of affection:

"I love you Facey. Happy Date Night"

His phone lit up immediately with a response:

"Thnx! Txt as many times as u like. Not all msgs go on screen. Txt ALERTS for Lakers News alerts. Msg&Data Rates May Apply. Txt STOP to quit. Txt INFO for info"

This wasn't what he expected. He was trying to surreptitiously arrange a scoreboard surprise for his date, but now his phone had beeped back at him. What if his companion thought that another woman was messaging him during their special evening? Frantically, he texted "STOP" to the Lakers. This boomeranged on him again, as the team felt the need to confirm this request with yet another text. "You will no longer receive messages or charges," it told him. It should have added: "And if Facey gets suspicious of this text, that's not all that you will no longer receive."

Emanuel could have seethed and stewed about the unwanted messages for several years, as his fellow Californian Jose Gomez had done when the Navy tried to enlist him. Instead, he quickly consulted an attorney and filed a class action TCPA suit. Never mind that the Lakers had two excellent defenses to the law. First, Emanuel had been the one who initiated the conversation, and the response was simply to let him know that his message might not be displayed. The team didn't want him and Facey to be disappointed when they watched the scoreboard all night and saw nothing but Gatorade ads. Second, it was implausible to say that the team had used an "automatic telephone dialing system" as the term is defined in the TCPA. The Lakers weren't dialing a list of numbers, but were instead sending individual replies as needed.

The lawsuit brought a wave of bad luck to the team, culminating with Kobe Bryant tearing his Achilles tendon the following April. And even when the judge dismissed the meritless case, the ordeal wasn't quite over. Emanuel filed an appeal, prompting the Lakers to negotiate a settlement with him. The team then fought its insurance company for several more years in an unsuccessful attempt to get it to reimburse the loss. Its policy did not cover "invasion of privacy" claims, and the 9th Circuit Court of Appeals narrowly agreed with the insurer that improper texting falls under that exclusion.

The Gen-Kal and Lakers cases show us that well-intentioned businesses can occasionally be hurt by inappropriate uses of the TCPA. But sometimes plaintiffs are branded as "vexatious" litigants in circumstances where the defendant isn't exactly operating with clean hands itself. We can look at examples like this in a couple minutes, but first we have to understand an influential case that was decided by the 7th Circuit Court of Appeals in 2012: Soppet v. Enhanced Recovery.

If there is one TCPA opinion that is worth looking up, reading in its entirety, and committing to memory, it is *Soppet*. It was written by Judge Frank Easterbrook, a conservative icon known for his incisive ability to cut through b.s. and make complicated legal concepts understandable. Indeed, this ruling is an extraordinary example of his well-reasoned prose.

Soppet concerned two separate plaintiffs from the Chicago area: Loidy Tang and Teresa Soppet. Both had acquired new cell phones at the start of 2007. Just like James Watson's haunted home from the previous chapter, these devices came with a bit of baggage. Their phone numbers were previously assigned to two individuals who had failed to pay their AT&T bills. Eventually, AT&T referred these past due balances to Enhanced Recovery for collection.

In October 2009, Enhanced Recovery began robocalling Tang in a misguided effort to resolve one of the bills. She would receive approximately twenty-nine prerecorded voicemails from the company. Soppet began getting similar spam messages in January 2010, and counted about twenty-five. They jointly filed a class action suit, but the collector raised the defense of consent. The previous users of the phone numbers had provided their information to AT&T, which (under the FCC's 2008 ruling) was enough to give its collector consent to call those numbers using automated equipment. However, the 7th Circuit needed to decide whether that permission also allowed innocent bystanders like Soppet and Tang to later be robocalled at these same phone numbers.

The TCPA permits automated calls to be made with the consent of the "called party." Enhanced Recovery argued that this phrase actually means "intended recipient of the call," but Judge Easterbrook declined to accept this attempted revision of the statute. He pointed out the other places in the law where "called party" clearly refers to either the current telephone subscriber or to the person who answers the call (who were usually one and the same). Nowhere does it mean "person who had that number three or four years ago."

Easterbrook also offered an apt analogy:

> "Borrower agrees with Bank, as a condition of a loan, that Bank can enter Borrower's garage and repossess his car if he does not keep current on payments. After signing this contract, Borrower sells his house, moves, does not tell Bank his new address, and defaults on the loan. Can Bank now enter the garage of the house where Borrower used to live and seize the car the repo men find there? Surely not. ... Similarly, Customer could consent expressly to receive calls at his current Cell Number, even if that number changes, but simply providing Creditor with a number—which is how Customer consented here—does not authorize perpetual calls to that number after it has been reassigned to someone else."

The ruling against Enhanced Recovery was not a surprise, because it was an especially unsympathetic defendant in several ways. First, it was trying to reach consumers who hadn't paid their phone bills and whose service had been disconnected as a result. Robocalling them at those same phone numbers was about as smart as launching a cable network for Amish TV viewers. Furthermore, Tang and Soppet both had voicemail greetings that identified them by name. If the defendant had ever called them with a live agent, it would have known immediately that the numbers were out of date.

Additionally, the company's bad habits were under fire from other victims around the country. The plaintiffs' counsel was flabbergasted to discover the extent of the wrongdoing. Enhanced Recovery had robocalled 3.5 million unique cell phone numbers in just the preceding six months, with virtually no evidence of consent. Many of the numbers had been obtained with skip tracing (or skip guessing) techniques. Even if Judge Easterbrook's ruling had gone the other way, most of these calls would have still been illegal.

Over the four-year period covered by the lawsuit, there could be as many as 25 million class members who were entitled to compensation. And yet, the defendant was a tiny enterprise with few assets other than a small insurance policy that would not be nearly enough to rectify the harm. It had also purged many of its records, making it impossible to identify everyone who would be eligible for a payment.

Despite these difficulties, the class action was settled. Soppet, Tang, and three other lead plaintiffs were each awarded $10,000. (Tang and Soppet also got a settlement from AT&T's Illinois subsidiary, which had authorized Enhanced Recovery's collection efforts.) The attorneys for the plaintiffs split $1.25 million, which represented nearly four years of work by seven law firms. The other millions of class members didn't receive any cash at all. They had to be content with an injunction that—in theory—would require the collector to start obeying the law. It was imperfect justice, but it was the best outcome under the circumstances.

There's little doubt that the defendant in *Soppet* richly deserved to be sued. However, the 7th Circuit's decision has helped pave the way for other cases that aren't so clear-cut. Sometimes a company has express consent to autodial a phone number for a legitimate reason, but then the number is transferred to someone with an extremely low tolerance for such disturbances. It may be impossible for the caller to know that the number has changed hands, and even one misplaced call can be enough to provoke someone into filing a TCPA claim.

Then there are those plaintiffs who *welcome* the wrong number robocalls. They know that each ring means another $500 in their pockets, and so they let the companies rack up twenty, thirty, or three hundred violations before they take any action. They might even take steps to attract more of these types of calls. As it turns out, there is a legal doctrine that applies to situations such as these. It centers on a provision of Article III of the U.S. Constitution:

> "The judicial Power shall extend to all Cases, in Law and Equity, arising under this Constitution, the Laws of the United States, and Treaties made, or which shall be made, under their Authority; —to all Cases affecting Ambassadors, other public Ministers and Consuls; —to all Cases of admiralty and maritime

Jurisdiction; —to Controversies to which the United States shall be a Party; —to Controversies between two or more States; —between a State and Citizens of another State; —between Citizens of different States; —between Citizens of the same State claiming Lands under Grants of different States, and between a State, or the Citizens thereof, and foreign States, Citizens or Subjects."

If you can see how this paragraph relates to robocalls, then you are way ahead of everyone else. In fact, you should probably be on the Supreme Court yourself. Head over there right now and ask to be fitted for your black robe.

As usual, the real meaning is not found in the words of the Constitution, but in how those words have been interpreted historically. When President George Washington wanted the Supreme Court to give him its opinion on an important matter, Chief Justice John Jay snubbed him. Jay pointed to the above paragraph from Article III, and said that the Court's job was only to decide cases and controversies. There had to be at least two adverse parties with an interest in the outcome, and issuing a mere advisory opinion was a waste of the Court's time. Get your attorney general to do that for you, George. That's why you have him.

Over time, the federal courts have further narrowed their interpretation of Article III. With just a few exceptions, they will only hear cases involving an "injury in fact." The plaintiff must have suffered (or is at imminent risk of suffering) some kind of actual harm that can be addressed by the courts. This was emphasized in the *Spokeo* ruling that was handed down by the Supreme Court in 2016.

In the *Spokeo* saga, it is Thomas Robins who plays the role of George Washington. Just like Washington, Robins is from northern Virginia. He has much else in common with the father of our country: he is a successful plantation owner, he is a devout Federalist, and he has wooden teeth. Actually, you can strike the last sentence; it's just a typographical error. But it contains the type of spurious information that you might have read about him on Spokeo, a website that offered free background reports on everyday Americans.

In 2010, Robins was—like many people that year—unemployed and looking for work. In an effort to understand why employers were ignoring his resume, he googled himself to see what his reputation was like. He discovered his Spokeo report, which got his name, address, and siblings' names correct. Everything else appeared to be a wild guess. It said he was an affluent married man in his fifties with children, a graduate degree, and a job in a professional or technical field. None of this was true. And as the cherry on top of the shit sundae, the report included a picture of a different person.

Robins filed a class action suit against Spokeo for violating the Fair Credit Reporting Act (FCRA) by disseminating inaccurate data. Under the FCRA's private right of action, he would be entitled to statutory damages of up to $1,000, plus legal fees and possible punitive damages. Spokeo argued, however, that Robins had not actually suffered an injury in fact. He couldn't prove that anyone else had even seen his Spokeo report until he had made a big deal about it by showing it to a lawyer. Besides, the misinformation was flattering in some respects. It isn't defamatory to say that someone is well-educated and financially successful.

Although the 9th Circuit Court of Appeals rejected this defense, the Supreme Court's institutional memory is long and unforgiving. It still resented how that nitwit George Washington had asked it to help him pick out a dress for Martha, or some other such silliness. Chief Justice Roberts was determined to use the federal courts' Article III powers sparingly as John Jay had done. He had little patience for a plaintiff who was angling for a cash award despite not being harmed in any way. Under his leadership the Court overturned the 9th Circuit's ruling by a 6-2 vote, and ordered it to reconsider its decision under more stringent guidelines. Robins would need to do a better job of proving an injury in fact.

Justice Ginsburg wrote the dissenting opinion. She observed that there was no point in having a do-over in the 9th Circuit, since it would be trivial for the plaintiff to show how Spokeo's inaccuracies can hurt him. An employer could mistakenly conclude from the background report that Robins is overqualified for a job that he wants. A potential girlfriend might read that he is married. Even if the harm couldn't be proven, the threat would always be present.

Ginsburg was correct that the remand was unnecessary. The plaintiff prevailed again in the rehearing, and Spokeo had little choice but to settle the suit. Robins could finally get back to doing the things that he loves, like crossing the Delaware and chopping down his father's cherry tree.

Despite the minimal impact that it had on Thomas Robins' case, the Supreme Court's *Spokeo* ruling was briefly a source of joy to debt collectors. They thought that it might put a new limit on TCPA lawsuits, because plaintiffs would now need to show that they were injured by the illegal calls. In the minds of these companies, everything is about money and so non-financial or "psychic" harm would not be enough. It was time to resurrect the old canard that a telephone customer must incur a charge for a robocall in order to have a valid claim for statutory damages.

Of course, this was still a nonviable defense. Congress, the FCC, and the courts have repeatedly recognized that unsolicited automated calls are a nuisance that the statute was designed to remedy. Any recipient who has suffered that nuisance has standing to sue. To ensure that the Article III argument won't result in the dismissal of a case, a civil complaint can simply include a brief statement of how the illegal calls have annoyed the plaintiff and interfered with his life. (It helps to use phrases such as "mental anguish," "embarrassment and humiliation," and "loss of sleep.") And for those who think that lawsuits should be filed only when there is a pecuniary loss, there is the cost of electricity to recharge a phone whose batteries have been depleted by the defendant's repeated calls. This minimal expense has actually been recognized by some courts as grounds for recovery under the TCPA.

Occasionally, though, a defendant can win by citing the *Spokeo* opinion. Consider the case of Melody Stoops, a clever Pennsylvania resident who devised a profitable enterprise based on the rule from *Soppet*. Beginning in 2014, she purchased at least thirty-five cell phones. She assigned them numbers from Florida area codes, knowing that the state had a large volume of people who were in financial distress. When one of the phones rang, it was usually an automated call from a collector who was trying to reach whoever previously had that phone number. Stoops kept a log of these calls while occasionally answering them and making half-hearted requests for the companies to cease communication. Periodically, she would sue a caller under the TCPA or send it a demand letter seeking a payment.

Wells Fargo Bank was one of the companies that fell into her trap. It called one of her phones an incredible 73 times in barely more than two months. It made 12 calls to another of her phones in the same time period. The bank stipulated that it had used an automatic dialing system for all of the calls, and so there was no question that it had done something illegal. However, it raised a defense that is unusual for a TCPA suit: assumption of the risk. This defense normally arises when someone is injured during a hazardous activity, such as skydiving, skiing, or eating unwashed romaine lettuce. Wells Fargo argued that Stoops had accepted—and even invited—the risk that she would get some of its robocalls. She had chosen to swim in dangerous Florida waters that she knew were infested by predatory lenders and obnoxious debt collectors, so she can't complain about being bitten.

Judge Kim Gibson didn't think that assumption of the risk was applicable to either the TCPA or to the facts of this case. However, the plaintiff had admitted in a deposition why she had so many phones that she never used for any purpose other than filing lawsuits. "It's my business," she said. "It's what I do." The judge was not enamored of this kind of "business," believing that it clogged the court system and made it harder for people to have legitimate disputes heard. He was determined to put a stop to it.

Relying on *Spokeo* and a number of other cases, Gibson ruled that Stoops did not have standing to pursue her claim. She had not suffered any injury, and her interest in collecting statutory damages was not what Congress anticipated when it enacted the law. The judge could have sent the case back to the state courts, which is where the plaintiff had first filed it before Wells Fargo transferred it to federal court. Instead, he chose to issue summary judgment in favor of the defendant, thereby ensuring that Stoops would walk away empty-handed.

No matter which way this case had been decided, the outcome was going to be unsatisfying. Stoops' business was certainly an inefficient use of the court's time, and she didn't merit a reward of tens of thousands of dollars. Despite that, she was still performing an important enforcement function that the FCC has mostly abdicated. Her shoebox full of cell phones had absorbed one of

Wells Fargo's shenanigans that would otherwise have marred someone else's quality of life. (The bank once allegedly harassed a Florida woman with 6,000 robocalls after she missed a mortgage payment.) In lieu of statutory damages, perhaps Stoops should be honored with a ribbon or a medal or something.

For a look at a case with a different outcome, let's turn back to New Jersey. In the same state where Gene Kalsky is fighting to stay out of the homeless shelter, another man is reaping the benefits of the TCPA. According to a 2017 series on *Forbes* magazine's website, entitled "Phoney Lawsuits," a disabled ex-construction worker named Jan Konopca has earned at least $800,000 in settlements by suing dozens of companies that robocalled him. It's fair to say that Konopca is a serial plaintiff, a term that is used disparagingly by *Forbes*, but there is more to his story than first meets the eye.

First, we have to reject the suggestion that "serial plaintiff" is automatically an insult. Consider Philip Charvat, an Ohio man who was one of the early pioneers in using the TCPA's private right of action to fight back against illegal sales calls. Think for a moment about the most common types of telemarketers who have ignored the Do-Not-Call list: alarm system vendors, TV satellite dish services, and travel agencies offering "free" cruises that wind up costing more than the ship. Charvat has sued all of these and more, and continues to do so whenever he has an opportunity. Besides collecting numerous judgments and settlements for himself, he has served as the lead plaintiff in several class actions that have benefited other consumers. This in itself is a testament to his character, because a court will usually disqualify someone as a class representative if it doubts his integrity or motives.

Furthermore, Charvat's aggressive tactics have generated some favorable case law that can be cited by others. Thanks to his efforts, Ohio courts have recognized that violations of the TCPA and its regulations—even the technical and procedural standards—can also be violations of the state's consumer protection law. This allows a victim of illegal robocalls to recover additional damages as well as attorney's fees. With contributions like this, Charvat is not just a serial plaintiff. As one judge wrote, seemingly with admiration, he is a "veteran litigant."

In terms of legal sophistication, Jan Konopca is no Philip Charvat. In fact, he didn't even seem to be aware of the TCPA until 2014. By that time he had received thousands upon thousands of unwanted calls over the preceding seven or eight years, and had responded with ineffective countermeasures such as reporting the callers to his local police. After finally taking the time to review his phone records with a lawyer, he filed thirty-one lawsuits in rapid succession. Many of the defendants settled quickly, leading to the reputed $800,000 figure cited by *Forbes*, but one of them decided to fight back with an Article III defense. FDS Bank (the credit card division of Macy's department stores) accused Konopca of "manufacturing" the TCPA claims much as Melody Stoops had done. In other words, he had suffered no injury from its automated calls and had no standing to sue the bank in federal court.

Konopca did not own thirty-five phones like Stoops did, but he did have three. One of these was assigned the number 222-2222. Verizon had given him this phone number for a landline in 2004 after he requested something catchy to use for his construction business. He credited it with helping him win customers who saw the memorable sequence of twos emblazoned on the side of his van.

Most small business owners would be grateful for such an effective promotional device, but this easy-to-dial number also carried a curse. It was a magnet for pranksters, drunks, and butt dialers. Any New Jersey housecat could easily knock its owner's phone off the hook and call Konopca to hiss at him. Debt collectors, especially, had an affinity for 222-2222. The number may have entered their robodialing systems in two different ways. For one thing, it was a convenient fake phone number for deadbeats to scrawl onto credit applications when they had no intention of honoring their commitments. Additionally, collection agents might have deleted incorrect phone numbers from their companies' databases by replacing them with a series of twos. Regardless of why the creditors were calling Konopca's number, they were never satisfied with making just one call. Each company bothered him dozens of times, often ignoring his demands that they stop.

As if that weren't enough to deal with, the audio quality on this phone line was pitiful. Verizon informed Konopca that the wire to his home was being eaten by squirrels and there was little that could be done about it. (It must be illegal to shoot squirrels in the Garden

State.) Frustrated by the technical difficulties, he switched to cellular service from Sprint in 2010. Sprint offered him three phones for the price of one, and he decided to keep 222-2222 on one of them. By this time Konopca had been hurt in a car accident and no longer did construction work, but he didn't want to lose the unique number that had become part of his identity.

FDS Bank's lawyers didn't believe that arboreal rodents were responsible for Konopca's decision to port his number to Sprint Wireless. They thought that he had done so because of the TCPA's stronger protections for cellular phones. This was the plaintiff's sinister way of laying a trap for the callers that had been harassing him. It was a trap that would have easily been avoided by checking the wireless portability database, as these companies were supposed to do, but it was a trap nonetheless. After changing phones he bided his time for four years, allowing the robocall violations to accumulate as he subsisted on his meager disability checks. Finally, his attorney cruelly pounced on the callers just before the statute of limitations expired.

This wacky conspiracy theory was even less credible than Verizon blaming squirrels for its poor landline service. If you believe that a disabled construction worker had the foresight and patience to execute this scheme, you probably also believe that Elvis faked his death just so he could see what his commemorative postage stamp would look like. However, the bank bolstered its argument with statistics. Konopca's phone records showed that 222-2222 received an average of eighteen calls each day, most of them probably spam. Meanwhile, he made only about three outgoing calls per month on that line since he preferred to call from his other two phones. It appeared as though he was keeping 222-2222 mainly so that he could attract TCPA violations. Since he barely used the phone for anything else, he had no right to claim that he was injured by the robocalls.

This would have been a laughable defense in any other context. It was like wrecking someone's car and then refusing to pay for the repairs because the owner didn't drive it much anyway. But in the wake of *Spokeo* and *Stoops*, Judge Peter Sheridan was obligated to give the bank's argument serious consideration.

FDS Bank hadn't made just an inadvertent robocall or two while it was on its way to volunteer at the soup kitchen. It had illegally called Konopca's cell phone 612 times, including 178 times in one monthly billing cycle in 2011. *Spokeo* or no *Spokeo*, the judge was disinclined to give the company much of a break. "Defendant has provided little or no evidence that it adequately monitored the calls to the 2222 number," he observed, while probably chuckling to himself at the extent of the understatement.

But Sheridan also wasn't convinced by the plaintiff's explanations for retaining a phone number that attracts so much abuse. Konopca said he liked having a simple number for his elderly mother in Poland to remember. It was likewise a convenient number to give to women who he met in bars. However, there was scant evidence of international calls to this line, nor did the ladies of the Jersey Shore seem anxious to dial a bunch of twos. Maybe women would be more likely to call the number if they knew about Konopca's $800,000 income.

"From a high level look, neither Plaintiff nor Defendant has a great factual case," the judge wrote. He concluded that Konopca was genuinely annoyed by the automated calls, and that he had probably complained several times about them to FDS Bank or Macy's. (This latter point was disputed.) In recent years, however, the plaintiff had shifted into a mode of sitting back and letting multiple companies rack up hundreds of violations. Sheridan refused to dismiss the suit, but suggested that the damages could be adjusted to account for any "manufactured" calls. The parties then agreed to a settlement, presumably for somewhat less than the $306,000 minimum statutory penalty.

The *Forbes* articles imply that Konopca is a greedy and abusive litigant. Whether that is true or not, he was clearly up against some greedy and abusive companies. It looks like he punched the bullies in the nose a little harder than they expected.

9. THE SCAM-BASED ECONOMY

You probably think we've covered the topic of scams already. What could be scammier than collecting donations for a non-profit group and then keeping 90% of them? Or demanding that someone pay an ancient bill, despite knowing that the debt is no longer legally valid? Or enticing Wells Fargo Bank into breaking the law, thereby damaging its pristine reputation, just to win a little cash in a settlement?

The fraudulent robocallers described in this chapter are different, however. They rarely concern themselves with the TCPA, the FCC, or other acronyms, because they believe they are beyond the reach of the U.S. government. You can find them in lawless no man's lands like the mountains of Pakistan, the ghettos of Jamaica, and the office parks of Florida. Anyone who sues one of these scammers will encounter insurmountable obstacles when trying to identify the defendants, serve a summons on them, and collect any judgment that a court has awarded. On the plus side, these callers are unlikely to raise any questionable defenses involving Article III of the Constitution.

Scams are, of course, as old as human history. Those who successfully perpetrate them are often the subject of admiration, while those who are cheated are mocked and scorned. As an example, consider Jacob from the Book of Genesis. His elderly father was about to confer the family blessing on his brother Esau, and this was a big deal. Getting the blessing was like being accepted into a top tier M.B.A. program. Esau would be set for life. But his dreams of a bountiful harvest, endless casks of wine, and a magnificent harem were all shot to hell when Jacob exploited their father's blindness to disguise himself as Esau and steal the blessing.

Jacob was clearly a scammer, yet it is he who is celebrated as the good guy in the story. Every grade school classroom today has five boys named Jacob and not one Esau. We justify Jacob's treachery by focusing on his brother's negative qualities. Esau was a monstrously hairy dude, for one thing. He was so hirsute that his brother had to cover himself in goat fur as part of his disguise. Also, he angered his mother by consorting with a couple of nasty Hittite women. A man like that deserved to be swindled out of his blessing and his birthright.

The Old Testament isn't the only setting in which fraudsters are lionized and their victims are shamed. In many films, the protagonist is a professional con artist. (*Catch Me If You Can*, *Dirty Rotten Scoundrels*, and *The Sting* are just a few of the memorable movies of this kind.) Audiences accept this type of leading man because he targets people who have more dollars than sense, and avoids hurting blameless third parties as part of his schemes. Grifters in movies have a strong work ethic and they usually channel all of their efforts into one big score. They are trying to pull off an inside job at a bank, or gain access to a billionaire's art collection so they can swap a priceless painting with a fake. They aren't going to waste their time hustling a naive tourist with a game of three-card monte.

Robocalling scammers are the antithesis of the dashing, heroic confidence men from Hollywood. They don't even rise to biblical standards of racketeering. They will gladly unleash a billion annoyances onto the public, not sparing anyone, just to locate a couple hundred clueless fools and take a small amount of cash from each. They are no more honorable or sophisticated than a crackhead who destroys a $5,000 air conditioner while stealing $10 worth of copper wire. It's unlikely that anyone will ever make a hit movie about a robocaller, because it will be very difficult to convince a major star to take that role:

> Agent: "George, I have a fabulous script for you."
>
> Mr. Clooney: "Is it one of those 'Ocean's' deals? What are we up to, 'Ocean's Twenty-Three'? I don't think we've robbed the Sioux tribal casino in the Black Hills yet."
>
> Agent: "No, the casino thing is worn out, thank heavens. Instead, you'll be playing the manager of a call center full of fake IRS agents. You and the supporting cast will spend twelve hours a day asking people to buy Apple gift cards to settle phony tax bills. Sweet, huh?"
>
> Clooney: "Do I drive a Lamborghini?"
>
> Agent: "Even better. Your character will have a Ford Focus. It gets exceptional mileage. And by the end of the film, he's

laundered so many of the gift cards that he can afford to remodel his kitchen."

Clooney: "I'm concerned we'll lose the male demographic. Not enough action. But if I keep my shirt unbuttoned the women might stay interested."

Agent: "Actually, the call center dress code is business casual. You'll be wearing comfortable but non-revealing polos and khakis."

Clooney: "How about if I just do another Japanese beer commercial?"

Most contemporary robocalls are, essentially, a variation of small dollar fraud. This type of crime used to be the exclusive realm of the embezzler, who was able to enrich himself slowly over several years. The typical small dollar embezzlement involved a cashier pilfering a few bucks here and there. Or maybe it was a General Motors worker taking a Cadillac home in his lunch box one piece at a time. (It didn't cost him a dime.) Only recently has technology allowed these types of thefts to be efficiently split among thousands, or even millions, of victims. Instead of stealing from one large company, the criminals can steal randomly from the public at large.

One of the first massively widespread small dollar schemes occurred in the late 1990s. It came to light when a family doctor in Minnesota, John Faughnan, reviewed his business Visa card statements from the previous few months and spotted multiple unfamiliar transactions for $19.95 apiece. He called the toll-free numbers that were listed next to the charges, but was never able to reach a live person. Visa was also of little help. Faughnan posted about the enigma on his personal website, and was soon inundated with hundreds of reports from others who were facing the same problem.

The Visa charges originated from several shadowy firms such as "J.K. Publications" and "MJD Services." As we have seen previously, businesses with monograms for names are often up to no good. (Sorry, IBM.) Faughnan traced these suspicious companies back to a common link: Kenneth Taves, a felon from California.

Taves was ostensibly in the business of operating pornographic websites. This was a lucrative industry in the 1990s, but he couldn't quite figure it out. His internet properties were getting even fewer hits than the GeoCities page of unusual mailboxes that your cousin photographed during her month-long vacation to Shreveport. Since users weren't signing up for his websites, Taves decided to sign them up himself. He requested a list of other people's credit card numbers from a bank, which oddly agreed to sell him this data despite his recent check fraud conviction, and soon obtained 900,000 new "members." Some of them noticed the charges right away and were able to get their credit card issuers to reverse them. The majority did not, however, and dutifully paid $19.95 each month. They probably thought it was a new tack-on fee from the cable company, or that the sun had been acquired by a commercial enterprise and everyone was now being billed for its use. Either would have been believable.

The FTC shut the operation down at the beginning of 1999, with the help of Dr. Faughnan's detective work, but the fun was just beginning. Over $37.5 million had been stolen, not counting another $7.3 million in unsuccessful charges that were attempted. The feds appointed a receiver to trace and recover the loot, a task that would take much longer than anyone anticipated. Millions of dollars had been transferred to the Cayman Islands. Millions more were in Australia, but had passed through the archipelago of Vanuatu on the way there. The government of that island nation insisted that the money was now theirs. (Be careful not to book any trans-Pacific flights that have a refueling stop in Vanuatu. They might put a lien on your luggage.) There were also a Cessna airplane and a $2 million mansion in Malibu. And Taves had apparently been suckered himself, frittering away $500,000 of the proceeds on a nearly worthless list of email addresses that he could spam with ads for his unappealing adult websites.

The scheme was costly for everyone involved. Two banks, including the one that had imprudently supplied the credit card numbers, went under. Taves was sentenced to more than eleven years in federal prison, and several accomplices were prosecuted as well. Long after Taves' release, the FTC and the receiver were continuing to scour the world's banking system for the last remnants of the stolen cash. Restitution checks were still going out to some victims as late as 2018.

After the Taves empire collapsed, it was several more years before similar large scale scams were adapted to telephone solicitations. The delay is surprising in retrospect, because all of the necessary pieces had been there for a long time. It was a mash-up of two bits of technology that would take telemarketing fraud to the next level. The first was the familiar automatic dialing and announcing device, which was used to deliver simple prerecorded messages like the ones Kathryn Moser had once used to advertise her chimney sweep service. The second was predictive dialing software, which attempts to route a call to an agent only when both parties are ready to speak. Pairing these two 1980s-era inventions produced interactive robocalls that could contact millions of people while efficiently weeding out those who weren't interested. Only the recipients who listened to the entire recorded spiel—and pressed the appropriate buttons on their telephones in response—would be connected to human representatives.

You'd have to look back several decades to find another serendipitous combination with this kind of effect on society. In the early 1960s, a McDonald's employee in Cincinnati impulsively slapped a piece of processed orange cheese onto a breaded cod patty that had done nothing to merit such an insult. Somebody served it to a customer before the distasteful mixture could be sealed in a lead capsule and buried in a landfill. It was the world's first Filet-O-Fish. As with interactive robocalls, the tragic innovation was unleashed onto the public with little concern for anyone's well-being.

For scammers, the new type of computerized call offered a benefit that was just as valuable as efficiency. It allowed an entire transaction to be completed in a single phone call made with a spoofed Caller ID. There was no longer any need to include a traceable return phone number in the recorded message. Fraudsters could now conduct their activities over the phone with almost complete anonymity.

Now that con artists had the necessary telephone technology, their goal was to formulate a sales pitch that would appeal to the truly desperate. Scams are most effective when they offer false hope to those whose lives have been torn asunder by intractable problems. Each generation has its own such difficulty that defines it. In the 1920s and '30s, when Dr. John Brinkley was advertising his unorthodox medical treatments, the biggest fear was impotence. An impotent man would be unable to sire the twelve or thirteen children that were needed for all of the farm and household chores. He would be willing to do anything to conquer this malady, even if it meant getting an organ transplant from a goat.

After World War II, the outward appearance of virility—symbolized by follicular health—replaced actual virility as the primary concern of middle age. Balding men became easy prey for those who were touting miraculous hair growth potions. Then the obesity epidemic was in full swing by the 1980s and '90s, probably due to the frequent contamination of otherwise wholesome foodstuffs by slices of processed cheese. Millions of people threw their money away on fad diet books and questionable weight loss programs. But in the new millennium, there is one problem that supersedes all of these others: the crushing burden of debt. Whether it be credit card purchases, student loans, or cars bought on eight-year installment plans, Americans of today love nothing more than having something now and paying for it later. And when "later" comes around, it's usually a crisis.

In 2005 and 2006, the first major wave of "lower your interest rate" robocalls stampeded across the United States and Canada. They were intended for those with credit card debt, though they were dialed indiscriminately. The callers had no idea which consumers carried a card balance from month to month, and often the calls were made to people who didn't even have a charge account at all. Murray Roman would have been appalled.

This campaign marked the debut of the world's first and only celebrity robocaller: Rachel. Little is known about Rachel's upbringing, her likes and dislikes, and her presumed vast financial holdings. She's never captured by the paparazzi while out clubbing with friends, and she never models a dazzling strapless gown on the red carpet at a robocalling industry awards show. Even her surname is a mystery, much like Madonna, Cher, and *Beyoncé*. Yet her voice has become part of the landscape of American life, along with abandoned malls, opioid abuse, and pointless arguments on the set of *The View*.

Rachel represents Cardholder Services, an organization that claims to work with credit card issuers to reduce people's financing costs. Those who take her robocall bait are transferred to an agent who engages in pleasantries and then requests a card number. The cardholder is then charged anywhere from a few hundred dollars to a couple thousand dollars and receives little or nothing in return. In the best case, one of Rachel's coworkers might call the person's bank and ask someone to knock the interest rate down by a couple of points. This is something that the consumer could have easily done by himself without adding a hefty new fee onto his balance.

The calls implicitly represent that Rachel has a connection with the consumer's bank, or even that Cardholder Services is a division of Visa or Mastercard. Her recordings assert that "there is no problem with your current account," as if she possesses inside information about the listener's spending and borrowing habits. When the human agent later asks for the call recipient's name and credit card number, it should be a red flag to people of average intelligence that Rachel and her team are not who she would like us to believe. But if you randomly select a group of ten people, usually eight or nine of them will be of below average intelligence. There are enough potential victims to keep Rachel occupied for a while.

When these calls began, Americans were angry but remained mostly calm. They knew that they could file a Do-Not-Call complaint with the FTC, or report the illegal robocalls to the FCC, and that the full weight of the law would be brought to bear. Rachel's cohorts would soon be trading contraband cigarettes with Ken Taves in the federal lock-up. Cardholder Services' ill-gotten proceeds would be seized and refunded to those who had stupidly given the scammers their credit card numbers. Then a tremendous fine would be imposed under the TCPA and the Telemarketing Sales Rule, ensuring that no one would dare try a stunt like this again.

The first strike against Rachel came from the FCC. In March 2007, it cited Cardholder Services, Inc. and its president Robert Pitsker for delivering unsolicited prerecorded sales calls to residential phones. Pitsker had incorporated Cardholder Services in 1991 and operated it from his home in southern California. The citation must have come as a huge surprise to him after a decade and a half in business without so much as a parking complaint from his neighbors. It was laughable to suggest that his little company had abruptly gone rogue and was now spewing out tens of millions of fraudulent robocalls. Indeed, his only connection to Rachel was that she had misappropriated his business' moniker in furtherance of her illegal scheme.

Fortunately, the FCC's action carried no penalty. None, that is, other than being incorrectly named and shamed as the source of the most hated telemarketing scam in history. The Commission permanently posted the citation on its website, making Pitsker and his company a target of abuse for years to come. As late as 2014, one internet commenter was still suggesting that the robocalls could be avenged by salting Pitsker's lawn or dumping fertilizer in his pool.

The FTC has been only slightly more competent than the FCC in its pursuit of Rachel. Each time it announces that it has shuttered the lower-your-interest-rate operation, it quickly winds up looking foolish. It can be likened to a police chief who confidently declares at a press conference that he's apprehended the hooligan who has been pooping on everyone's doorstep. The wicked fiend is now behind bars and there is nothing more to fear. Then the moment the chief exits the building, he hears a sickening squishing sound beneath his feet. Either the police have arrested the wrong person, or else copycat poopers have discovered that doorsteps are an unexpectedly profitable location to leave their deliveries.

The FTC's ineffectiveness can be traced to its enforcement tactics, which have weakened considerably over the past two decades. When it learned of the J.K. Publications credit card fraud in 1999, the Commission demanded $37.5 million in restitution from Ken Taves and referred him to the Justice Department for criminal prosecution. It then dispatched its minions to the ends of the earth to retrieve the money. Today the FTC's usual response to a scam is to negotiate with the offender on friendly terms, as if buying a lamp from him at a garage sale, rather than treating him like the scoundrel that he is. The typical settlement is something like:

> "Judgment is hereby entered against the defendant in the amount of $22,516,382. This judgment is permanently suspended due to the defendant's inability to pay, on the condition that he kindly abstain from the placement of additional unlawful telemarketing calls. The defendant also agrees to surrender specified assets, including a genuine Franklin Mint Civil War Chess Set (missing two Confederate pawns and Union queen Clara Barton) and a Chipotle gift card that probably has a couple bucks left on it. If the defendant is later found to have misrepresented his financial condition, the Commission is going to be really pissed but probably won't do anything."

With this sort of punishment being the only deterrent, it is no surprise that the lower-your-interest robocalls are continuing to this day. If you aren't using a call blocker you've probably answered two or three of them since you began reading this chapter. The recording of Rachel is starting to wear out after being played a few trillion times, so some of her friends are helping with the announcements. This raises a hopeful possibility for eventually cracking the conspiracy. If, say, Heather from Account Services is ever captured and threatened with waterboarding, she might be persuaded to give up the goods on Rachel and the others.

There are few remaining suckers who have yet to hear the Rachel script, and so these calls are not the big money-maker that they once were. The con artists could probably get a better return on their investment by converting their call centers into Blockbuster Video stores. But even when they were scoring the big bucks a decade ago, Rachel and her friends had the good sense not to get too greedy or to flaunt their wealth. That's what tripped up one of the largest robocall operations of the late '00s.

In 2008 and 2009, it seemed as though everyone's vehicle warranty was about to expire at the same time. It didn't matter whether you drove a sparkling new Lexus or a thirty-year-old prison van that you rescued from a junkyard. Everybody knew that their warranties were in danger because of the frequent automated phone messages that told them so. The callers offered the opportunity to purchase an extended maintenance plan that would supposedly protect car owners from unplanned breakdown costs. While there are no hard statistics to prove it, it's likely that these robocalls briefly surpassed the lower-your-interest scam as the primary use of the nation's telecommunications system. The phone companies couldn't install fiber optic cables and cell phone towers fast enough to keep up with them.

One of these calls reached the mobile phone of Senate Majority Leader Chuck Schumer, interrupting him while he was attending an important meeting on Capitol Hill. Harassing the senior senator from New York was like poking a bear with a stick. It wasn't like poking a grizzly bear, which would have provoked a forceful response. It was more like poking the docile, heavily tranquilized bear from the Snuggle fabric softener commercials. Schumer denounced the robocalls and complained that the government wasn't doing anything about them. Too bad that he didn't know anyone in a position of power and authority who might have been able to address the problem.

The FTC did shut down a Florida company, Transcontinental Warranty, that it blamed for many of the calls. However, this was just one piece of the puzzle. An even bigger scheme was underway in Missouri, signified by a nine-bedroom mansion that was rising suspiciously in a modest middle class subdivision along the south shore of Lake Saint Louis. The new house had a bowling alley, a movie theater, a beauty salon, an infinity pool, and many other fine amenities that were unheard of in St. Louis area homes. Why would anyone need these entertainment options when they already had a 600-foot arch that they could look at for free?

The home was to be occupied by Darain Atkinson. Along with his brother Cory, Atkinson had started an auto warranty company that quickly grew to become one of the region's biggest employers. The firm was now on its third name: US Fidelis. Its name and branding evoked the concepts of loyalty and fidelity. This was appropriate, because the company's board of directors was extraordinarily loyal and faithful to the Atkinson brothers. It routinely authorized payments of millions of dollars to them, including nearly $27 million to construct Darain's castle. The money came from the reserves that were supposed to have been used to cover claims filed by purchasers of the warranties.

US Fidelis owed its success to deceptive direct mail campaigns and, later in its existence, deceptive and illegal robocalls. This wasn't a recipe for sustained customer satisfaction, and by 2009 there were more people cancelling warranties and demanding refunds than there were signing up for new policies. The company's finances collapsed and its bankruptcy trustee put the lakefront home on the market. The Atkinsons had been efficient with their money by not paying taxes on much of it, but they should have shopped around for more affordable construction materials. Darain's mansion could be sold for only $4.75 million, a fraction of what it had cost to build, and that was after sweetening the deal with a couple of boats and several other vehicles. Cory's relatively modest bungalow, which had been built for $10 million, yielded another

$2.8 million for the bankruptcy estate. Most of the money owed to customers, vendors, and investors was never to be seen again.

It took several years, and consumer losses in the range of eight or nine figures, but the government won the battle against the two worst vehicle warranty robocallers. The Atkinson brothers ultimately went to prison for fraud, as did two of the executives at Transcontinental Warranty. You may have noticed that the TCPA did not even make an appearance in this fight, even though it was disobeyed repeatedly by both of these enterprises. The threat of billions of dollars in civil penalties was of absolutely no consequence to the swindlers and those who assisted them.

It's obvious why no one bothered to pursue a class action TCPA suit against the car warranty scammers. After the fraud victims were partially reimbursed, there certainly wasn't any cash left over for anyone else. But as it turns out, there is sometimes another obstacle to using the law's private right of action to fight con artists. It is illustrated by the 2017 ruling in Spiegel v. Reynolds.

This case came about when an Illinois man, Marshall Spiegel, was repeatedly bothered by robocalls seeking donations for the Breast Cancer Society. He knew that charities were allowed to make these types of calls to landlines, thanks to the various exemptions in the TCPA, so he figured he was just going to have to tolerate them. Plus, suing a group that was gathering money for cancer patients was not something that would endear him to the rest of the world.

But then the FTC announced that the Breast Cancer Society and three related organizations weren't charities at all. They were actually a "massive, nationwide fraud" perpetrated by James Reynolds, Sr. and his extended family. Over $187 million of donations had been collected between 2008 and 2012 for medications, hospice care, and supplies for those who were ill. By and large, however, the money was spent on trips to Vegas and Disney World, jet ski outings, dating services, cruises, concert tickets, and other perks for Reynolds' relatives. More than 97% of it was wasted on these types of benefits, along with fundraising costs and other expenses unrelated to the groups' stated missions.

And what about the 3% that wasn't wasted? It was squandered. Instead of the promised medical supplies, the "charities" bought random junk from overstock warehouses and then shipped it to cancer patients. A typical package might contain a DVD of a

Christian movie, a few disposable plastic utensils, a couple odd-sized clothing items, and some Moon Pies. The groups would then file misleading statements with state regulators and the IRS, claiming the original retail value of the items as charitable expenditures when in fact they had bought them at a deep discount. One of the organizations, the Cancer Fund of America, apparently couldn't find enough sick people who wanted their homes cluttered with boxes of useless crap. So the Fund unloaded the parcels onto various non-profits around Knoxville, Tennessee, such as a youth soccer league, a firefighters' association, and several churches and senior centers. The whole time, it was telling donors that their money was being used to assist patients all over the country.

In a rare show of unity, the attorneys general of every state and the District of Columbia joined the FTC in filing a complaint that would shut the sham charities down. Given the dollar amount of the alleged fraud, and the cruel exploitation of a worthy cause, you are probably guessing that the government exacted a harsh penalty from the individuals who were involved. That isn't what happened. Judgments totaling $136 million were imposed against three of the defendants, which seemed like a good first step. However, all but $135,000 of the penalty was suspended due to their supposed inability to pay. And, unlike the Ken Taves and car warranty cases, no one went to prison.

Upon learning of the FTC's complaint and the lenient terms of the settlement, Spiegel decided to pursue a TCPA claim. The calls to him had been made by Associated Community Services (ACS), a fundraising firm that worked closely with the fake charities. It pocketed 85% of the incoming donations even before they could be misspent by the Reynolds family. ACS had somehow escaped the Commission's wrath and was still an ongoing business, so it made a viable target for a class action. Spiegel also sued three of the individuals who had operated (and personally enriched themselves from) the Breast Cancer Society. His theory was that the calls were not entitled to the TCPA's non-profit exemption, for obvious reasons.

Spiegel's case went nowhere. Judge Edmond Chang wasn't interested in exploring the details of the Society's finances to decide whether it was truly a non-profit. That type of inquiry would tread dangerously close to the practices that had been ruled unconstitutional in the *Schaumburg*, *Munson*, and *Riley* cases. The Society had called itself a charity in its IRS paperwork, and this assertion would be accepted regardless of what the plaintiff (and the FTC) thought of it. Besides, the judge noted that even for-profit companies are allowed to call landlines—including those on the Do-Not-Call list—if they don't solicit for the purchase of goods or services. Sales robocalls are forbidden by the TCPA, but it's OK to take people's money while offering them nothing in return.

Chang's ruling saved ACS from possible bankruptcy and liquidation, allowing it to continue soliciting for other clients after the Reynolds enterprise was shut down. Its dubious activities on behalf of one of them, the Foundation for American Veterans, would lead to ACS being temporarily banned from fundraising in Minnesota. The Foundation is now defunct, but if you are a military veteran you can be assured that plenty of similar "non-profit" organizations are looking out for you. You can anticipate a crate of Moon Pies, plastic sporks, and religious DVDs in the mail soon.

There is one law that was enacted specifically to combat the scams discussed in this chapter: the Truth in Caller ID Act of 2009. It makes it illegal to "knowingly transmit misleading or inaccurate caller identification information with the intent to defraud, cause harm, or wrongfully obtain anything of value." The FCC is authorized to fine offenders immediately without first giving them a warning citation. A violation of the act can also be prosecuted as a crime, with a sentence of up to a year in prison for a first offense.

Senator Bill Nelson of Florida introduced this measure at the start of the 111th Congress in January 2009, proposing to add it as a new section of the TCPA. Punishing those who fraudulently spoof Caller ID information seemed like an obvious idea, and no one of either party objected to it. And yet, the bill languished in committee. Perhaps it fell on the floor underneath a desk, remaining there for eons until a senator rediscovered it while looking for an Altoid he had dropped. Eventually it was passed unanimously by the Senate and sent to the House for more languishing. It wasn't signed into law by President Barack Obama until the waning days of the session in December 2010, at which time it seemed untruthful to still call it the "Truth in Caller ID Act of 2009."

Although Nelson and his colleagues took forever to cook up this law, it came out of the congressional kitchen looking like someone forgot to turn on the oven. It was missing the spicy ingredient that made the rest of the TCPA so tasty: a private right of action. Enforcement was left mostly up to the FCC, and it was complicated by the act's vague language. What does it mean to "cause harm" or "wrongfully" obtain something? Without a private right of action, there would be few—if any—court decisions to interpret these words.

The FCC didn't penalize anyone under the act until 2016. When it did, its target was not a robocalling scammer as one might expect. It was a man from New York who had used a Caller ID manipulation service and a voice modulator to anonymously annoy a friend's ex-wife. He spoofed the phone numbers of Sing Sing and other correctional facilities, and informed the woman that there was a prison cell waiting for her. The man was fined $25,000 despite his protestations that he had no intent to "cause harm." He was just goofing around with a few hilarious prank calls.

In 2017 and 2018, the FCC finally decided to make an example of three high-volume robocallers who had used spoofed Caller IDs. A home improvement service in Arizona was ordered to pay $37.5 million. The owner of a small insurance agency in Wilmington, North Carolina was fined $82.1 million. But the biggest penalty was assessed against Adrian Abramovich of Miami, the man who would be crowned by the media as the "King of Robocalls."

Abramovich specialized in selling travel packages over the phone. He had been ignoring the Do-Not-Call List for many years, with little hassle from the authorities, but his latest endeavor had ruffled the feathers of some important birds. His automated calls disrupted a medical paging network, prompting the pager company to complain to the FCC. Also, the robocall messages claimed to offer discounted vacations and reward points from some of the giants of the tourism industry, such as Hilton, TripAdvisor, and Marriott. In truth, none of these companies wanted anything to do with Abramovich or with the miserable Mexican timeshares that he was promoting. The scheme unraveled when one of the calls reached TripAdvisor's lead fraud investigator, who feigned interest in the offer and persuaded an agent to give out some revealing information.

The FCC accused Abramovich of making 96,758,223 illegal robocalls, but that figure covered only the last three months of 2016.

In fact, the calls had been going out for a year or more prior to that time. They used a technique known as "neighborhood spoofing," in which the Caller ID information was changed dynamically for each call so that it would match the area code and first three digits of the recipient's phone number. The Commission took a random sample of 80,000 of the calls and verified that each and every one contained an incorrect Caller ID that was generated in this manner. It proposed a penalty of $1,000 for each call in the sample, and then modified it upwards by 50% based on Abramovich's prior history of violating the TCPA and on his general "egregiousness." The $120 million fine was the largest that the agency had ever issued, far eclipsing those meted out for unlicensed broadcasts, interference with police radios, and televised wardrobe malfunctions.

But the fine wasn't the worst of it. Abramovich was also ordered to testify before the Senate Committee on Commerce, Science, and Transportation on April 18, 2018. The senators were likely expecting the King of Robocalls to be a sneering, defiant villain like one from a Batman movie. Instead, they got a modest man with a strong Argentinian accent who didn't look much like a king of any kind. He didn't even look egregious. Mostly, he looked worried as the lawmakers expressed their strong disapproval of his actions.

Senator Ed Markey was one of those who berated the reluctant witness. Markey recalled his role in writing the TCPA in his youthful House of Representatives days, and proudly referred to it as "my law." He was not happy that *his* law had been so callously disrespected.

"Mr. Abramovich," Markey said, "you represent nearly one hundred million reasons why we need robust protections from the epidemic of robocalls and robotexts afflicting the nation." He went on to explain that any robocall was a disturbance and an invasion of privacy, even if it lasted only a minute and could easily be dismissed. "Do you understand why it irritates people? Do you understand why they don't want these unwanted calls, Mr. Abramovich?"

"Yes, I understand," the marketer meekly replied.

Although Abramovich acknowledged the senator's frustration, he didn't seem to think that any of it was his fault. He lamented the state of the telemarketing industry, and noted that even he—the alleged "King"—receives four or five robocalls a day. But the problem, in his view, was not that the regulations are too lenient; it was that they are too strict. He traced the rise in robocalls to a change that the FTC made to the Telemarketing Sales Rule.

Prior to the rule change, telemarketers were more apt to work from a list of leads that were gathered in unclear and usually devious ways. These leads were people who had supposedly requested more information about a type of product or service. If the telemarketer was later accused of breaking the Do-Not-Call rules, he could point the finger back at the company that had sold him the leads. The marketer was told it was a list of individuals who enjoyed learning about travel opportunities. How was he to know that they really didn't want to hear a sales pitch for a diarrhea-filled vacation at a substandard resort?

The value of lead lists diminished in 2009 when the FTC began to require companies to get advance permission in writing for all sales robocalls. Telemarketers could no longer rely on questionable lists for plausible deniability. There was only one logical thing to do: ignore the lists altogether and abandon any pretense of following the law. Why not robocall *everyone* by randomly dialing every phone number in existence? Of course, some of those numbers might belong to fraud investigators who entrap the telemarketer and cause him to get fined millions of dollars. In this way, Abramovich believed he was a victim of the times too.

As of yet, the $120 million has not been paid. Abramovich and his attorneys have advanced several arguments as to why it shouldn't be. One is that the amount of the penalty is so extreme as to trample the constitutional rights of due process and protection from excessive fines. The FCC retorted that it could have been a lot worse. If it had levied the maximum fine, and counted all the calls rather than the sample of 80,000, the total would have exceeded $1 trillion. The Commission observed:

> "The fact that even a greatly reduced per-violation forfeiture amounts to $120 million is a problem wholly of Abramovich's own making. Abramovich elected to engage in massive spoofing and committed more than 96 million separate violations. The volume of his violations does not justify a 'volume discount.'"

Abramovich raised another defense: he is a telemarketer, not a scammer. Sure, his robocalls dangled the promise of a luxurious stay at a top-notch hotel, only to deliver a mandatory condo sales presentation in the basement of the Puerto Basura Motor Lodge. But he was just trying to make a living as a salesman, and some puffery was to be expected. The elements of a Truth in Caller ID Act violation were not met because he had no intent to defraud anyone or to cause harm.

The FCC rejected this argument and pointed to the various ways that the calls had caused harm. They had infringed the trademarks of respected travel services, thereby misleading consumers and damaging the companies' goodwill. They had crowded legitimate traffic off of wireless networks and had produced a backlash against those whose phone numbers were hijacked for use in the spoofed Caller IDs. And, fundamentally, the mere act of annoying someone with an unwanted robocall was causing harm. All of these ill effects were the obvious consequence of Abramovich's calls, and he can't say that he didn't intend for them to happen.

With this response in May 2018, the FCC signaled that it would be interpreting the Truth in Caller ID Act very broadly. After reaffirming the $120 million penalty, Chairman Ajit Pai decided to crow a little bit about the Commission's newfound fortitude:

"This is the largest forfeiture in the history of the FCC. Our decision sends a loud and clear message: this FCC is an active cop on the beat and will throw the book at anyone who violates our spoofing and robocall rules and harms consumers."

But while the chairman was patting himself and his colleagues on the back, Commissioner Jessica Rosenworcel poured a big bucket of seawater down everyone's pants:

"If you think the number of robocalls you receive is going up, you're right. We're drowning in them. Last month there were 3.4 billion robocalls nationwide. That's one third more robocalls than during the same month last year. This is insane.

"Today the FCC adopts a forfeiture order imposing a penalty on one operation that made tens of millions of robocalls two years ago. I support it. But let's be honest: Going after a single bad actor is like emptying the ocean with a teaspoon—and right now we're all wet."

She then enumerated the ways in which the government was failing both consumers and businesses on other matters concerning the TCPA. There was plenty to gripe about. Let's rewind a few years and look at why she was so dissatisfied.

10. CONFUSION ALL AROUND

Author's Note: This chapter discusses some of the most actively debated current issues surrounding the TCPA. It's a little heavier on the legal stuff than some of the others, so I will be only mildly angry if you skip it. The rest of the book will still make sense without it.

As the TCPA celebrated its 20th birthday in 2011, it was under attack from all sides. Robocallers had long exploited its loopholes, but now some of them seemed impervious to the law altogether. The public was getting angrier by the week at all of the nuisance calls from Rachel and her friends, and enforcement actions by the FCC and FTC were few and far between. Only another dramatic speech by Fritz Hollings could save America from this menace. Unfortunately he had long since retired, leaving the Senate to a bunch of boring John Barrassos and Amy Klobuchars who just wanted to debate appropriations bills and judicial nominations.

Meanwhile, business groups had an entirely different perspective. They were increasingly worried by the hazards that the law presented to anyone who needed to contact consumers via voice, text, or fax. The unwarranted "Facey" suit against the Los Angeles Lakers would soon confirm their fears of how a well-intentioned outreach campaign could blow up in an organization's face. In response to this threat, the U.S. Chamber of Commerce began to actively lobby for "reform" of the TCPA to make it friendlier to legitimate businesses. Among other changes, the Chamber recommended ending strict liability, putting caps on damages, and cutting the statute of limitations to one year. Any of these modifications would, however, have made it even tougher to deter the scammers, telemarketers, and debt collectors who were defying the law.

When corporate interests spoke, Representative Lee Terry of Nebraska listened. He introduced the Mobile Informational Call Act of 2011 (MICA), which he said would modernize the TCPA and allow businesses to more easily communicate with their own customers. He gave a couple of examples of how his proposed law would improve our lives. For example, parents would be able to give their cell phone numbers to a school district and then receive a robocall or text whenever there was a snow day. Banks could make automated calls to consumers when their checking accounts were close to being overdrawn. Terry claimed that those practices were somehow illegal under the existing version of the TCPA.

Terry lined up ten cosponsors for MICA. One of them, Representative Marsha Blackburn of Tennessee, said that the new law would permit FedEx to send package delivery notifications to its customers. The only Democratic cosponsor, Representative Ed Towns of New York, praised Terry for introducing MICA. Towns believed that the act would somehow create jobs and reduce the deficit. He stopped short of arguing that it would bring about peace in the Middle East or allow NASA to land astronauts on Venus.

Terry's bill seemed headed for quick passage, but then a funny thing happened: people actually read it. They learned that MICA didn't just tweak the TCPA, as its sponsors had suggested. It practically gutted it. MICA would remove all automated commercial calls, other than telemarketing solicitations, from the bounds of regulation. It would bring back the annoying predictive dialers that the FCC had restricted in 2003. It would redefine "prior express consent" to include situations that were more like implied consent at best. And, finally, it would ban states from enforcing their own restrictions on robocalls and robotexts.

Public interest groups realized that MICA was a Trojan horse. It was being promoted as a way to let valuable information be efficiently delivered to consumers, but the reality was vastly different. In particular, the bill would legalize debt collection robocalls to cell phones, regardless of whether made to the debtor or to a third party. (Several collections industry trade groups had signed on as supporters of the legislation.) Strangely, however, Terry wasn't touting spam calls from FDS Bank and Wells Fargo as one of the benefits of his bill.

On November 4, 2011, the House Committee on Energy and Commerce held a hearing on MICA at which several representatives aired their concerns. Anna Eshoo said she had received numerous letters opposing the bill. Henry Waxman pointed out that useful robocalls from school districts and businesses were already legal, with proper consent, and he questioned why a change to the law was needed. Joe Barton observed that opening up cell phones to reasonable automated calls would inevitably lead to unreasonable ones coming through as well. Mike Doyle said he had recently purchased a washer and dryer, and he didn't want the store to use his phone number for any purpose other than telling him when the appliances would be delivered. John Shimkus expressed relief that Doyle would finally be wearing clean clothes.

The committee heard from several witnesses on both sides of the issue. The star of the panel was Indiana Attorney General Greg Zoeller. He told the representatives that his state was very happy with its strict laws against automated calls and telemarketing, which the new bill would pre-empt and replace with much weaker federal restrictions. He warned them that Indiana was not going to give in to the robocallers without a fight. The AG didn't say it directly, but the passage of MICA could very well lead to a second Civil War. The congressmen shuddered at the thought of a rebel Hoosier army, led by Colonel John Mellencamp, Marshal Larry Bird, and General Greg Zoeller, marching to Washington and ransacking the Capitol.

The hearing ended with the committee agreeing that MICA's stated intent was laudable, but that the bill needed some revisions. Republicans and Democrats vowed to cooperate on a rewrite. This didn't happen, though, and they instead let the measure die quietly without a vote. In 2014, Nebraska voters rewarded Lee Terry's brilliant work on MICA by booting him out of Congress and letting him take a higher paying job as a corporate lobbyist. He seemed better suited for that role anyway.

It was a shame that the Chamber of Commerce had overreached with MICA, because a couple of its gripes about the TCPA were quite valid. One was that the definition of an "automatic telephone dialing system" (ATDS) was still a little vague. Wall Street hates uncertainty more than almost anything else, so this was not an ideal situation. Here's an experiment you can try if you are a CEO: just use the word "uncertain" somewhere in the next report to your shareholders. For example, "The uncertain tariff regime will mitigate our ongoing service revenue in the first quarter, resulting in a higher than expected carry forward surcharge." A statement like this will invariably cause your stock price to plummet the next day, even if no one knows what the heck you are talking about. If you also toss in the phrase "potential class action litigation," investors will be jumping out of windows.

Everybody knew that a predictive dialer qualified as an ATDS, thanks to the FCC's 2003 ruling, and that it could not be used to call cell phones without consent. The next best option for efficiently calling a large number of people is a "preview dialer." It presents each phone number to an agent via a computer screen, and he or she must then click a mouse button to initiate the call. It was generally believed that preview dialers were legal because this type of system has no capacity to dial a list of numbers without repeated human intervention. (Remember that the word "capacity" is critical to the definition of an ATDS.) However, companies that used these devices still sometimes found themselves targeted by TCPA lawsuits. A verdict could depend on the technical details of the equipment, the relative strengths and weaknesses of each side's expert witnesses, and the whims of a judge. Often it was safest just to settle.

Business interests were eager for the FCC to give preview dialing devices its blessing so that the cloud of uncertainty would be lifted. But each time it was asked for its opinion, the Commission simply pointed back to its previous rulings. It didn't want to appear to endorse a particular product, and it definitely didn't want to inadvertently create another loophole. If all preview dialers were decreed to be legal *per se*, someone would certainly find a way to abuse the privilege. Imagine overseas sweatshop workers rapidly making simultaneous calls by blindly pushing buttons on a preview dialer, only to have those calls put into a predictive queue for handling by agents in the United States. The result would be a system with all the same flaws as a predictive dialer—including all of the hang-up calls—except that it would have an FCC stamp of approval.

You might not believe that anyone would invent a bizarre Rube Goldberg-style contraption just to exploit a perceived gap in the TCPA. Yet, a hybrid preview-predictive dialer wouldn't be the stupidest such innovation. That dishonor belongs to something called "ringless voicemail," which allows callers to leave a prerecorded message in a voicemail mailbox without first ringing the associated mobile phone.

The difference between a conventional robocall and a ringless voicemail is like the difference between an obscenity shouted from a car window and a bag of manure thrown from the same window. A fleeting insult can be ignored, but you have to physically clean up the manure. Also, you don't know what's in the bag until it opens and you get the contents all over yourself. It's much the same way with a ringless voicemail. Without seeing a Caller ID number on your phone, you have no idea whether the message might be important until after you have wasted a couple of minutes retrieving it.

So why would anyone, other than a malicious telephone vandal, send ringless voicemails to someone without that person's authorization? Probably because a vendor has convinced them that the messages don't qualify as wireless calls under the TCPA. A ringless voicemail is sent, in many cases, via a landline number that belongs to a customer's cellular provider. The cell company must maintain this number for technical reasons, but it also provides an exploitable back door into the voicemail system. Some spammers believe that they are following the letter of the law (while utterly flouting its spirit) by playing their prerecorded messages over these landline connections and avoiding any direct calls to consumers' phones.

There are two problems with this legal theory. The first is that it has yet to be endorsed by the courts, which so far have seen voicemails as essentially the same thing as calls or texts. After all, the net result is much the same: a notification is sent to a wireless phone, and an automated message is delivered. The FCC has also not weighed in on the matter, and doesn't appear likely to give the ringless voicemail spammers any kind of break.

The second problem is that there are a few technical limitations on this technique, meaning that it doesn't work for all types of wireless telephone customers. It is also prone to being cut off at any time when cellular companies catch on to how their systems are being abused. So, some ringless voicemail calls are actually made with a different method that requires two steps. First, an automated dialer calls the targeted individual's cell phone and then disconnects within a fraction of a second. The goal is to hang up before the phone rings, but a partial ring is often heard. The autodialer then initiates a second call to the same number while the person's line is still tied up by the first call. The second call is routed straight to voicemail, where the electronic signal is converted into the audible equivalent of a bag of manure.

This latter delivery method has some negative implications for companies who haven't bothered to get permission before sending a ringless voicemail. For one thing, it requires *two* forbidden automated calls to be dialed for each message. Double your penalty, double your fun. The evidence then appears in phone records and in the recipient's voice mailbox, where it can be conveniently preserved for use in court. Furthermore, ringless voicemail doesn't usually function with landlines, so anyone who employs it is effectively admitting that they willfully and knowingly targeted wireless phones. That improves the odds of a plaintiff winning triple damages for each of the two violations. This is how a single unsolicited voicemail can explode into a $3,000 claim.

As you can see, ringless voicemail is a nuisance to recipients and a potential financial catastrophe for senders. Even at its best, it is about as useful as a sneeze guard on a urinal. At its worst, it deserves a special exhibit in the Hall of Terrible Inventions, alongside internet popup ads, unnecessarily long shoelaces, and diluted vodka. What will its creators think of next? Perhaps they will breed a new type of mosquito that can spread acne from one person to another.

The FCC's silence on preview dialers, ringless voicemail, and other technologies was a concern for businesses. The bigger worry, however, was the "prior express consent" that is required for virtually all automated calls and texts to mobile phones. Obtaining authorization to call a customer was not too hard, but maintaining it over time was a challenge. Let's consider an example of how consent works in the non-TCPA world.

Suppose you have a generous friend who hands you a key to his pickup truck and invites you to borrow the vehicle whenever you please. It's implicitly understood that your friend has the right to retract this permission at any time and for any reason. This isn't just a rule of social interaction; it's a firmly established common law principle. If you return the truck with a flat tire, an empty gas tank, and a live alligator sprawled across the seats, you might lose your borrowing privileges and there isn't much you can do about it.

Sometimes, however, revocation of consent can be unclear. Perhaps your friend is too polite to say that he no longer wants you driving his truck, so he merely drops a few unsubtle hints. ("I sure hope my F-150 doesn't get another flat any time soon. It's hard to change a tire since that gator bit my arm off.") Or maybe he sells the vehicle without informing you, and then the new owner calls the police when you see it parked at the mall and decide to take it for a spin. An arrangement that was once so simple has now turned into a legal quagmire.

Consent works much the same way for automated calls as it does for trucks, except that it usually arises from a consumer transaction rather than a friendship. Just like friendships, these types of customer relationships often sour at some point, usually when the purchaser has decided to stop making the required payments on the product. After receiving repeated robocalls hounding him for money, he inevitably tires of the repeated disruptions and wishes to revoke his permission for the company and its bill collector to call him. Most people agreed that withdrawal of consent was possible under the TCPA, but there were disputes about how it should be done. Some businesses thought that the consumer needed to write a formal letter of revocation, translate it into five languages, and hand deliver it to the company's general counsel. Some consumers thought it was sufficient to yell "Shut up!" at a recorded message that was playing over the phone. Courts tried to find a consistent rule somewhere in the middle, but usually it came down to the facts of each case.

Meanwhile, reassigned phone numbers were a constant threat to even the most honest and diligent of enterprises. For example, many stores had a list of loyal customers who loved getting text messages about their latest clearance sales. They didn't realize that some of those customers had switched phone numbers, often because they regretted giving out their information to marketers, and that their advertising was now going to people who hadn't asked for it. Since the TCPA is a strict liability statute, the businesses could be—and often were—sued for these errant texts.

The FCC was constantly besieged by petitions from corporate lobbyists hoping for clarifications of the TCPA and for relief from liability for calls to reassigned numbers. Finally, in the summer of 2015, the Commission responded with a ruling that answered many of the concerns. However, its answers weren't what business groups wanted to hear.

The Commission affirmed what many courts had already decided: consumers were free to revoke consent for automated calls, and could do so "using any reasonable method including orally or in writing." This wasn't a terribly controversial statement, but it prompted some grumbling. Santander Consumer USA, a lender whose heavy-handed collection practices frequently ran roughshod over the TCPA, had urged the FCC to either require revocation to be in writing or disallow it altogether. Santander's unhappiness with the ruling suggested that the FCC had made the right call.

But the Commission seemed to struggle when it came to reassigned numbers. It recognized the quandary that businesses were facing, since there was no way to know with complete certainty when a phone number was switched to a different customer. (The telecommunications vendor Neustar offered a service that could help callers detect many such reassignments, but it acknowledged that it was "not a silver bullet.") On the other hand, the National Consumer Law Center (NCLC) cautioned against opening up a loophole that would be abused. It noted the large volume of complaints that had been filed with the Consumer Financial Protection Bureau against irresponsible debt collectors who robocalled the wrong parties again and again, often providing no convenient way for the recipient to stop the calls. Many of these incidents, such as the famous *Soppet* case, stemmed from reassigned numbers.

The FCC settled on a compromise that made no one happy. It created a "safe harbor" rule that would protect companies from liability for their first call to a reassigned number. After that first call, the caller would be deemed to have actual or constructive knowledge that the number now belonged to a new subscriber and that any previous consent was no longer in force.

Business groups were outraged that this was all the protection that they got. What if no one answers their safe harbor call? It would go to waste. They complained that they needed at least a year's worth of calls to detect the reassignment of a phone number. The NCLC, however, pointed out that the TCPA didn't give the FCC any authority to issue even the very limited one-call exemption. It could only allow unsolicited calls to cell phones when they didn't cause an expense for the consumer. These safe harbor calls would, in some cases, result in unwanted charges.

The truly disastrous part of the 2015 ruling, however, was the FCC's clumsy effort to clarify the definition of an ATDS.

Businesses had been hoping for some guidance as to how much automation they could get away with before their dialing systems posed a litigation risk. All they wanted was for someone to tell them that their preview dialers were OK. Some reassurances about their texting systems would be nice too. But once again the Commission sidestepped the automation question, and chose to instead dwell on its favorite word: "capacity." Recall the language that Congress wrote back in 1991:

> "The term 'automatic telephone dialing system' [ATDS] means equipment which has the capacity to store or produce telephone numbers to be called, using a random or sequential number generator; and to dial such numbers."

The FCC had already viewed the word "capacity" somewhat broadly, allowing it to include predictive dialers within the scope of its ATDS regulations. Now, in 2015, it emphasized that the word means something more than just "present ability." It encompasses potential future capabilities as well. For example, you might not have the present ability to run a marathon but you probably have the *capacity* to do so. All it takes is completely changing your lifestyle, diet, and exercise habits. By the same token, almost any computer-based dialing platform has the capacity to be an autodialer if appropriate software is installed.

The Commission's explanation was consistent with the dictionary definition of the word, and it wasn't dramatically different from what it had said in its predictive dialer ruling of 2003. With the technological changes that had happened since then, however, it took on a more ominous meaning. Any iPhone or Android phone can be easily modified to dial random or sequential phone numbers by downloading an app. Since every smartphone has the capacity to function as an autodialer, every call made with one was now potentially subject to liability under the TCPA.

This was obviously not what the FCC intended, and yet it stubbornly refused to clear up the confusion. Even when challenged by Commissioner (and later Chairman) Ajit Pai in his dissenting opinion, the majority of the commissioners were not convinced that there was a problem with the language they chose. They brusquely dismissed his concerns:

"... [T]here is no evidence in the record that individual consumers have been sued based on typical use of smartphone technology. ... We have no evidence that friends, relatives, and companies with which consumers do business find those calls unwanted and take legal action against the calling consumer. We will continue to monitor our consumer complaints and other feedback, as well as private litigation, regarding atypical uses of smartphones, and provide additional clarification if necessary."

The FCC's ruling was supposed to provide broader protections to consumers while also offering greater clarity to businesses. As we shall soon see, it backfired spectacularly on both counts. But 2015 was only half over, and there was more turmoil on the way. This time the blame would rest with Congress.

For several years, the Department of Education had been suggesting a supposedly painless way to reduce delinquencies on federally guaranteed student loans. What if private collection agencies could use robocalls without restrictions when working these government debts? Some bureaucrats had the fanciful belief that this would reduce the deficit by tens of millions of dollars each year. The idea was dismissed at first, but then the controversial provision was tacked on to the must-pass Bipartisan Budget Act of 2015 during a closed-door congressional conference. The TCPA was amended to include the new exemption when President Obama signed the budget into law.

Several members of Congress expressed outrage when the change came to light. However, no one would admit to slipping it into the bill. It was like the scene at a party when the hostess finds her guests standing around a broken antique vase, with all of them disclaiming any knowledge of how the destruction occurred. Perhaps the vase simply reached the end of its natural lifespan, one of the onlookers suggests, while another guest offers to run to Wal-Mart for some Scotch tape. The vandalism of the TCPA yielded a similarly unhelpful congressional response. Measures to repeal the ill-considered exemption were immediately proposed but then only half-heartedly pursued.

This special immunity for federal debt collection contractors damaged the TCPA's content-neutrality and opened the door to new

First Amendment challenges. We'll look at those shortly. Meanwhile, several business groups filed suit to block the FCC's ruling, claiming that the agency had abused its discretion when interpreting the statute. The organization leading the charge was ACA International, which represented the interests of the collection industry. Collectors had long been the TCPA's biggest enemy, and the events of 2015 gave them an opportunity to weaken and discredit the law.

The challenge to the FCC's order would take several years to resolve. During this time, it posed an obstacle to TCPA enforcement as defendants would frequently ask courts to defer their own cases while it was pending. But when the Court of Appeals for the District of Columbia Circuit handed down a decision in ACA International v. Federal Communications Commission on March 16, 2018, its ruling didn't quite tie everything up neatly in a gift-wrapped package. In fact, it only added to the mess.

The *ACA Int'l* opinion was written by Judge Sri Srinivasan, a universally respected jurist who was once on President Obama's shortlist for the Supreme Court. (The honor of being nominated for the promotion, only to be strung along for months without any action by the Senate, instead went to his colleague Merrick Garland.) Srinivasan and the other two judges on the panel were in agreement that the FCC's 2015 ruling went way too far:

> "It is untenable to construe the term 'capacity' in the statutory definition of an ATDS in a manner that brings within the definition's fold the most ubiquitous type of phone equipment known, used countless times each day for routine communications by the vast majority of people in the country. It cannot be the case that every uninvited communication from a smartphone infringes federal law, and that nearly every American is a TCPA-violator-in-waiting, if not a violator-in-fact."

The court also complained that the Commission had offered contradictory explanations of the "essential functions" of an autodialer. Did a dialing system need to be able to "dial random or sequential numbers" to be classified as an ATDS? Must it "dial numbers without human intervention"? Did it require the capability to "dial thousands of numbers in a short period of time"? The FCC had equivocated on all of these points.

Judge Srinivasan and his peers couldn't tolerate the Commission's ambiguity, so they decided to substitute an ambiguity of their own. They decreed that the FCC's attempts to define an ATDS were "set aside." Unfortunately, they didn't clarify whether they were setting aside only the 2015 order, or whether they were also throwing out the FCC's previous restrictions on predictive dialers that the agency had enacted in 2003 and reiterated in 2008. Either interpretation of the court's ruling was equally plausible.

Given the fuzzy outcome, *ACA Int'l* was like a Rorschach inkblot test for TCPA attorneys and their clients. Plaintiffs' lawyers argued that the ruling merely restored the status quo prior to 2015. It certainly wasn't a victory, but at least now all of the lawsuits that were on hold could finally proceed. Defendants and their attorneys, however, insisted that the decision was a turning point. Fifteen years' worth of pro-consumer regulations and case law had been doused with gasoline and set ablaze. Blow the dust off of those predictive dialers and let the spamming begin anew!

It was up to federal district courts across the country to interpret the ruling. Some agreed with plaintiffs that *ACA Int'l* was limited in its scope, and that most automatic dialers were still covered by the regulations. The courts that didn't accept this argument were faced with a major challenge. They needed to interpret the wording of the TCPA from scratch, while disregarding all of the guidance that the FCC had provided over the years. It turned out that the statute's definition of an ATDS was just as perplexing as some of the Commission's pronouncements.

The key bone of contention was the phrase "random or sequential number generator." Most TCPA defendants called people who were on a particular list of debtors or potential customers. They didn't generate phone numbers at random, and they almost never sequentially trolled through a telephone exchange like the kid from *WarGames* did. Although there was little doubt that most of these companies were using automatic dialing equipment that initiated all calls with computer software, there was a question as to whether these dialers met the peculiar requirements that Congress had laid out. In other words, a system that selects and dials phone numbers without any human intervention may—oddly enough—not qualify as an automatic dialer under the law.

In the early years of the TCPA, it was generally believed that a list-based autodialer couldn't be classified as an ATDS. This limited view of the law began to fall out of favor when the FCC broadened its regulations in 2003. The few people who clung to it were regarded as extremists or kooks. They probably also thought that the Federal Reserve should be abolished in favor of the gold standard, or that we should bring back the ducking stool as a punishment for disorderly women. But sometimes progress goes around in circles rather than following a straight line, and now in 2018 this antiquated opinion was being welcomed back into the mainstream. For some companies that had been accused of illegally making autodialed calls, it was the only defense that they had. They might as well give it a try.

It is possible for two different courts to examine the ATDS definition under a microscope, subject it to a thoughtful analysis, and arrive at opposite conclusions on this issue. As our first example, consider the case of Binyamin Pinkus of Chicago. He seemed like the type of urbane man who would enjoy listening to music, sports, and Howard Stern on a satellite radio. Sirius XM's telemarketing vendors simply couldn't believe that he would turn down their subscription offers, so they repeatedly called him with a list-based predictive dialer, texted him, and even left him several prerecorded voicemail messages advertising the service. In total, they contacted him over one hundred times.

Sirius XM was already settling a $35 million class action for this type of behavior, but Pinkus knew that—given the large number of violations he had experienced—he would be better off suing the company on an individual basis. However, *ACA Int'l* threw a wrench into his plans. Judge Gary Feinerman declared that the FCC's predictive dialer regulations were no longer in effect as a result of that ruling. Furthermore, he determined that list-based dialers were outside the scope of the TCPA since they did not generate random or sequential phone numbers. He rejected most of Pinkus' case, leaving only his claims for the prerecorded messages.

Less than two months after *Pinkus* was decided, the 9th Circuit Court of Appeals offered its take on the same question. The 9th Circuit case has its roots in 2012, when Jordan Marks signed up for a membership at Crunch Fitness in El Cajon, California. The club then began sending occasional marketing text messages to him, which increased his phone bill since he did not have an unlimited plan. As a positive, though, the unwanted texts served as good reminders to get to the gym for a work-out. He was probably motivated to hit a punching bag for a couple of hours after receiving each one. Following the third such incident, Marks decided to turn Crunch Fitness into his own personal punching bag by initiating a class action TCPA suit.

The plaintiff would be in for a bumpy ride through the legal system. First, the district court judge ruled that Crunch's texting system wasn't an autodialer because it had no present or future capacity to dial random or sequential phone numbers. Marks filed to overturn the verdict, but then the subsequent ruling in *ACA Int'l* appeared only to strengthen the defendant's case. Finally, he had an unlucky draw at the 9th Circuit. His appeal would be heard by three conservative appointees of President George W. Bush who were deemed likely to treat his lawsuit with hostility and derision. Let's hope he held on to that gym membership, despite all the text spam, because he was going to need to run a few miles on the treadmill every day to take his mind off of the stressful litigation. However, the outcome was surprising.

In its opinion written by Judge Sandra Ikuta, the 9th Circuit reached the same initial conclusion as the *Pinkus* court: *ACA Int'l* had overturned all of the FCC's guidance about automatic and predictive dialers. That would ordinarily be good news for the defendant, but the appellate panel didn't stop with that observation. It then proceeded to parse the ATDS definition that was in the TCPA, and concluded that every possible interpretation was problematic.

An ATDS must have "the capacity to store or produce telephone numbers to be called, using a random or sequential number generator." The rules of English require the phrase after the comma to modify both verbs: "store" and "produce." The difficulty is that it is not really possible to store phone numbers with a random or sequential number generator. It's a preposterous notion, sort of like eating a sandwich with your elbow. Courts were struggling to resolve this paradox.

In the *Pinkus* case, Judge Feinerman claimed to have found the one and only true answer to the conundrum. He thought the number generator requirement modified the noun "telephone numbers" rather than the two verbs. Put another way, a dialer is an ATDS only if it calls numbers that were randomly or sequentially generated. But plaintiffs such as Marks believed that the number generator requirement must apply only to the verb "produce." If their view was correct, then any system that dialed from a stored list would be restricted by the law.

Judge Ikuta and her colleagues recognized the futility of these grammatical exercises. The statute was simply ambiguous, and no amount of toying with the wording and punctuation was going to change that. The 9th Circuit panel instead looked at other parts of the law to figure out what Congress was thinking. It observed that companies were allowed to use an ATDS if they had advance consent from the people that they were calling. A-ha! Obtaining consent would be impossible if they were just making up phone numbers at random. Therefore, an ATDS must be able to dial from a list of known numbers.

This view was reinforced by the exemption that was surreptitiously added to the Bipartisan Budget Act of 2015. If the TCPA wasn't intended to cover the list-based dialers that collectors use, then the collectors wouldn't have needed this loophole. By adding the exemption, Congress had effectively acknowledged and ratified the expansive definition of an ATDS that was recognized at the time. This probably wasn't what the anonymous congressperson intended when he snuck the provision into the budget bill. The intoxicating influence of campaign contributions from the financial industry must have impaired his judgment.

Crunch Fitness pondered an appeal to the Supreme Court, but ultimately backed down and agreed to settle the lawsuit. That leaves *Marks* as one of the most influential rulings of its kind. Like *Soppet*, it is recommended reading for anyone who wants to gain back the IQ points that they lost while reading this book. And yet, despite the 9th Circuit's persuasive reasoning, several other courts around the country have issued opinions that conflict with *Marks*. The consequence of all this is that using an autodialer to call someone without their permission may or may not be legal, depending on where that person lives and which judge is assigned to the case. Care to take a gamble?

The D.C. Circuit's big *ACA Int'l* decision of 2018 didn't just invalidate the FCC's guidance about automatic dialers. It also threw out the Commission's one-call safe harbor for calls to reassigned numbers. The court felt that this rule was "arbitrary and capricious," which is judge-speak for "someone pulled it out of their butt." But the end of the safe harbor was no great loss, because the FCC had by this time begun working on a reassigned number database. When fully implemented, it will allow callers to avoid the liability risk altogether. Whether organizations take advantage of it, or blow it off like so many of them have done with the wireless portability database, remains to be seen.

Although *ACA Int'l* eviscerated the FCC's 2015 ruling in two important ways, it did uphold its handling of revocation of consent. Recall that the Commission authorized consumers to withdraw consent by "any reasonable method," similar to what is allowed under the common law. But once again this wasn't the end of the story. Let's consider a familiar example, but with a new wrinkle.

Suppose you have a generous, but hungry, friend who suggests that you buy him lunch. If you do so, he promises to let you borrow his pickup truck whenever you please. He will soon regret the free meal because he has just entered into a binding contract with you. Unlike in the previous truck scenario, he can't withdraw his permission on a whim or even for a very good reason. He is stuck with the deal until the day he no longer has a vehicle to lend. That's probably the same day that you carelessly leave the truck in gear and it rolls into the Hudson River, or it gets impounded because you used it to smuggle narwhal tusks across the Canadian border.

As robocall lawsuits began piling up in the early 2010s, many lenders and merchants added TCPA-specific fine print to their agreements with consumers. For example:

> "As an essential part of the consideration for the Purchase of __One (1) Genuine Leather Recliner That Will Disintegrate in Two (2) Years__, and for the extension of Favorable Credit Terms of __35.99% APR payable Monthly for Five (5) Years__ in connection with said Purchase, Purchasor authorizes Purchasee and its agents, assigns, and successors to

perpetually make, transmit, or otherwise deliver telephone calls, text messages, and voicemail recordings to any Telephone Number(s) owned, controlled, or used by Purchasor, regardless of whether a prerecorded voice, artificial voice, or automatic telephone dialing system is employed. Purchasor agrees to immediately notify Purchasee of any change to such Telephone Number(s) and to indemnify and hold harmless Purchasee of any damages suffered as a result of Purchasee calling Innocent Third Party ____fifty-two (52)____ times after Purchasor moves to ____Chattanooga____ without telling us. Enjoy the shitty ____chair____."

This is an even more one-sided deal than the one your friend negotiated. He will be free and clear of obligations once you wreck his truck, but the consumer who signs the above agreement will be getting robocalls long after his recliner has gone to the living room in the sky. And even though the FCC said that consent can be withdrawn, and the D.C. Circuit agreed with this position in *ACA Int'l*, several courts have ruled that the law of contracts supersedes this right of revocation. Now you have one more reason to never, ever buy anything on credit.

The disputes over autodialers and consent used up a lot of bandwidth in the federal courts in the 2010s, while leaving the rules just as unclear as ever. Worse still, the TCPA's constitutionality was in doubt once again. Now that federal debt collection contractors had special immunity to the statute, several political groups and pollsters were challenging the law as an unfair content-based restriction on their First Amendment right to free speech.

The debt collection loophole was troubled from the beginning. It compared unfavorably with several other tweaks that were made to the TCPA regulations around the same time. For example, the FCC gave a break to freight companies who wanted to send package delivery notifications to customers. It also allowed banks to send automated fraud alerts, and permitted health care providers to make robocalls containing important medical information. Few people had any objections to these useful types of robocalls and robotexts. It was important to know immediately that UPS had left an item on your porch, for example, since it meant that you had forty-seven seconds to get home from work before it was stolen. These three exemptions were reasonable extensions to the existing rules about consent and emergency calls, and there were strict limits on them to prevent them from being abused.

Unlike the other exemptions, the new rule for debt collectors originated with Congress rather than the Commission. The FCC then ran into pushback when it tried to set some boundaries as it had done for the other types of callers. It proposed limiting the collectors to three automated calls a month and refusing to waive their liability for wrong number calls. Collectors complained that this would defeat the whole purpose of the loophole. They were *supposed* to be able to hound debtors repeatedly and embarrass them by also robocalling family and neighbors. Commissioner Ajit Pai was disgusted with both the exemption and his colleagues' attempt to wallpaper over it with new rules, saying that the process had turned the TCPA into "a dog's breakfast." Ultimately the Commission backed down after Pai became the chairman, and its limits on the loophole never went into effect.

The 4th Circuit Court of Appeals reviewed the political organizations' First Amendment complaint and gave its opinion in April 2019. It readily determined that the new loophole was a content-based restriction. A company could make two nearly identical collection calls, one for a commercial loan and one for a government-backed student loan, and would be penalized only for the commercial one. Since the exemption authorizes "many of the intrusive calls that the automated call ban was enacted to prohibit," it made the entire statute under-inclusive. The TCPA now failed the "strict scrutiny" test that is applied by the courts in free speech cases such as this. It was unconstitutional.

But the 4th Circuit noted that the law had been "fully operative" for twenty-four years prior to the addition of the loophole. It didn't want to throw Fritz Hollings' beautiful baby out with the polluted bathwater. It instead chose to strike down the exemption for government debt collectors while keeping the remainder of the statute in force. The 9th Circuit would issue a similar opinion two months later in a case in which Facebook tried to get the TCPA declared unconstitutional. (Thanks a lot, Zuckerberg.)

These rulings were a Pyrrhic victory for the political groups who had challenged the TCPA. They had been hoping that the courts would overturn the entire law and authorize unlimited robocalls, robo-polls, and robo-fundraising. It would be the first step toward a brave new world in which automated politicking will totally supplant the old way of doing things. Politicians will eventually be able to send robotic avatars out to give speeches, shake hands, and commit gaffes on their behalf. The age of cyberpolitics will give birth to a new breed of scandals; perhaps the Hillarybot will be caught using itself as an email server. And yet, despite all of these advances, the machines still won't be allowed to call cell phones.

The decisions by the 4th and 9th Circuits are consistent with a common theme of the TCPA in the 2010s: almost every action has had unintended consequences. The FCC tried to make its rules tougher, only to have a court knock them back to the Stone Age. The D.C. Circuit tried to clarify the FCC's regulations, but instead disturbed everyone's longstanding assumptions and triggered a wave of contradictory rulings across the country. Congress tried to weaken the TCPA with a loophole, but then the 9th Circuit used this new exemption to help justify an expansive reading of the law. That's three branches of government, and three goals scored on the wrong end of the field.

Will the future of the law be much better? Probably not. Let's take a look at what's coming up.

11. THE CRISIS ENTERS ITS 4TH DECADE

Currently, at the end of the 2010s, the volume of spam robocalls is estimated at billions per month. They now comprise roughly half of all telephone traffic. But it isn't just the quantity of the calls that has attracted renewed attention to the problem; it's the increasingly malevolent nature of them.

The lower-your-interest-rate scams, the bogus travel offers, and the bottom feeder debt collectors are all still there, but are getting harder to find amid a massive deluge of impostor calls. Now there are fraudsters who brazenly impersonate law enforcement officers as part of their extortionist schemes. No agency is immune: the FBI, the IRS, local courts, and immigrations officials are all fair game. Next there will probably be calls mimicking the elderly security guard at the public library, telling us we have an overdue book fine that must be paid by sending Bitcoins to Romania.

America's blue chip companies are not safe from impersonation either, as evidenced by the callers claiming to represent "Microsoft technical support." Clusters of automated scam calls also frequently disrupt operations at hospitals. One such incident struck Tufts University Medical Center in Boston—right on Senator Ed Markey's home turf. Spoofers have even hijacked the FCC's phone number for use with their illegal activities, as if deliberately mocking the agency's powerlessness. Unsolicited robocalls were always a nuisance and a threat to public safety, but now they represent something else: the utter humiliation of the United States and its institutions. A nation that possesses eleven aircraft carriers and a million prison cells has proven to be no match for a few low budget con artists.

Now that robocalls have caused most of us to stop answering the phone, the real danger is that we are not receiving important communications. The *New York Times* recently reported on a New Jersey hand surgeon who faced a huge influx of spam on his cell phone and began ignoring incoming calls from numbers that he didn't recognize. That's how he missed hearing about a severed thumb that urgently needed to be reattached, causing one person's very bad day to be made even worse. What could be more unpleasant than sitting in the E.R. for two hours while waiting for a doctor? Sitting in the E.R. for ten hours while waiting for a doctor, and anxiously guarding your Igloo cooler the whole time to keep someone from mistaking your thumb for their lunch.

When the TCPA was enacted in 1991, some feared that it would infringe on First Amendment rights. Ironically, the far greater threat to free speech has instead come from those who break this law or who unfairly exploit its exemptions. In the marketplace of ideas, those with the biggest mouths and the smallest thoughts have foreclosed an entire avenue of communication for anyone who might have something worthwhile to say. FCC Commissioner Geoffrey Starks offered a concise summation of the crisis in a 2019 statement:

> "I've said it before and I'll say it again, robocalls have changed the fabric of our culture—if you get a call and don't recognize the number, you don't pick it up. Often, calls are spoofed to look like they are coming from a local business or neighbor. This pernicious practice makes it so we can't differentiate these unwanted robocalls from calls from our doctors or our kids' schools. Put simply, by allowing these calls to proliferate, we've broken phone service in this country."

It was technology, in the forms of automated calling equipment and cheap and untraceable voice-over-IP connections, that created the catastrophe. Technology will be needed to remedy it. The FTC realized this in 2012 and began sponsoring a series of contests for inventors to find the best way to tackle the problem. One of the inaugural winners was Nomorobo, created by entrepreneur Aaron Foss, which has become one of the best known call blocking services. Numerous similar products and apps are available today, including RoboKiller, Hiya, and Allied Interstate Obliterator. (OK, maybe one of these doesn't exist yet, but there's always hope.)

The success rate of call blockers is often advertised as 90% or better, but any boastful claim like this always comes with an asterisk. It's reminiscent of a bathroom cleanser that supposedly "Kills 99.9% of germs!" What about that other 0.1% of germs that can survive being doused with bleach? They are the most dangerous microbes of all, and they are going to be really ticked off that you tried to kill them. And so it is with robocalls: those that get past the blockers are usually the ones that are the worst. They use spoofed Caller IDs stolen from random telephone users, they route their calls through international switches to defeat any attempts at tracing, and they compensate for the blocking efforts by ramping up their efforts and doubling or tripling the number of calls.

The fundamental problem with all of the call blocking tools is that they focus on the wrong end of the equation. Robocalls would be better handled at the origin, and this is where the government and telephone providers have failed us in every possible way. However, there may finally be a little bit of progress on the horizon, as the FCC is urging the adoption of the Caller ID validation protocol known as STIR/SHAKEN. (Many people call it SHAKEN/STIR because they would rather sound like James Bond than be precise.) With this new technique, each call will receive a cryptographic certificate that confirms its origin. Spoofing of Caller IDs will become more difficult and call blockers will become more effective.

Already, some experts are cautioning us not to get too excited about STIR/SHAKEN. One limitation is that it won't work for calls coming from outside the United States and Canada. Also, some of the smaller phone companies in the U.S. appear to have cobbled together their landline networks using cables and capacitors they salvaged from Alexander Graham Bell's old laboratory. Asking these technologically backward companies to implement public key cryptography is a non-starter. It might provoke them to exit the industry and burn all of their equipment for the insurance money, which would leave their customers without phone service. So, there will continue to be legitimate phone calls that can't be validated with STIR/SHAKEN, and this raises questions as to how they can be accepted into the phone system without opening up another pathway for the bad guys.

As for the TCPA, Congress is planning some additions to it. The Telephone Robocall Abuse Criminal Enforcement and Deterrence (TRACED) Act, introduced by Senator John Thune of South Dakota, includes the following measures:

- The FCC will be able to levy a civil forfeiture against robocallers without first issuing a warning citation. The statute of limitations for actions by the Commission will be increased to three years for intentional violations. (For the private right of action, it will remain four years.)

- All phone companies must implement STIR/SHAKEN, and the FCC must allow blocking of numbers that haven't been authenticated.

- The attorney general, the FCC, and other government agencies must join forces to figure out how in the heck everything got to be such a mess and what can be done about it now.

- The FCC must consider restricting the availability of phone numbers to keep them from falling into the hands of scammers.

The House of Representatives is considering its own measure that is tougher and far more thorough than the Senate's. The Stopping Bad Robocalls Act (SBRA), sponsored by Representative Frank Pallone Jr. of New Jersey, includes several features that are missing from the TRACED Act:

- The FCC must clarify the definition of an "automatic telephone dialing system" to ensure that it can't be easily evaded. Its regulations must also guarantee that consent for automated calls and texts can be revoked.

- The FCC must revisit its existing exemptions to the TCPA, including the infamous 1992 loophole that allows most types of undesirable robocalls to be made to landline phones without consent. The Commission must limit who can place these calls and how often they can do so.

- The meaning of "called party" is clarified to remove any lingering doubts about whether *Soppet* was rightly decided. Also, the FCC's reassigned number database is given Congress' blessing.

- Phone companies must provide robocall blocking free of charge to consumers and small businesses.

- Retention and sharing of information about robocalls between voice-over-IP service providers, the FCC, and the Department of Justice will be improved. The FCC will be required to report fraudulent robocall schemes to the attorney general for criminal prosecution.

- The FCC and law enforcement will be ordered to go after "one-ring" scams in which a quick hang-up call is made with a foreign Caller ID to trick someone into responding with a toll call.

- The FCC and FTC must convene a "Hospital Robocall Protection Group" to defend the nation's healthcare facilities from the scourge of automated calls.

Both of these bills are wildly popular. The TRACED Act passed the Senate by a vote of 97-1 on May 23, 2019. SBRA passed the House on July 24, 2019 by 429-3. Now a conference committee must work out the differences between the two, pay homage to lobbyists from the debt collection industry, and produce a watered down version for final passage. To save you the trouble of looking it up, here are the four members of Congress who refused to support the proposals:

Senator Rand Paul of Kentucky. He also temporarily blocked funds for 9/11 victims, and he was assaulted by a neighbor whom he had angered by repeatedly dumping debris at the edge of the other man's yard. The senator's opposition to the TRACED Act is, quite obviously, part of his effort to earn the coveted title of Most Disliked Lawmaker in the United States.
Representative Justin Amash of Michigan. He's determined not to let Senator Paul win that trophy without a fight.
Representative Andy Biggs of Arizona. He complained that SBRA would give up too much of Congress' authority to "unelected bureaucrats" at the FCC. This is a valid concern, so

Biggs is undoubtedly working on a much better bill that will clean up the robocall epidemic without relying so heavily on the Commission. We're waiting, Mr. Congressman.

Representative Thomas Massie of Kentucky. He has a rare illness that prevents him from voting "yes" on anything. The disease has progressed to the point that he even opposed naming a post office after Maya Angelou. Massie and his constituents need our prayers.

The TCPA (and these possible extensions to it) is still of serious concern to companies who have built their entire existence around telephone spam. However, many of them don't seem to realize that the law is no longer the biggest risk to their business model. Today they face an existential threat from the changes in personal communications habits and the increasing availability of call blocking services. To contact a millennial, you don't call him or her on the phone unless you are part of a small cadre of very close friends and family. Making an uninvited call to a mere casual acquaintance is now treated as a faux pas—like wearing a Speedo to a funeral—if you can even get through at all. Organizations that rely on the phone for outreach must adapt to the new reality, in which voice calls have been replaced by social media. Otherwise, they will perish.

Under these constraints of technology and etiquette, how will the Association of Bosnian-American Police Lieutenants find new donors? Maybe they can set up a profile on a dating app. ("Our turn-ons include bimonthly pancake breakfasts, anti-marijuana presentations to senior citizens, and outrageous fundraising fees. Swipe right to support us.") How will creditors let people know they have an unfulfilled obligation? They can post nasty comments on the alleged debtors' vacation photos. ("Looks like you had a great time in Madagascar. Now please tell everyone how you can afford a $5,000 trip when you still haven't paid your dentist bill from 1997.") These maneuvers will be sure to get everyone's attention.

The obvious difficulty with using social media in this way is that every website and app has Terms of Service that prohibit spam and abuse. Facebook, Tinder, and LinkedIn don't tolerate activities that drive their users away and cost the companies some of their advertising or subscription revenue. Those who engage in this conduct in cyberspace are banned, filtered, and shunned. And now, with the FCC (and probably Congress soon as well) endorsing call blocking at the carrier level, phone services are about to become more like internet application providers. Their relative success at protecting subscribers from undesirable interruptions will turn into a competitive advantage. In this environment, the TCPA will scarcely even be a factor when deciding which calls and texts should get through. They will be subject to blocking if they are deemed to be a nuisance, even if they are entirely legal.

    This doesn't mean that the TCPA is becoming irrelevant, or that the time we have spent learning about it will go to waste. For all its numerous faults, and despite all of the damage unwittingly inflicted on it by the FCC and the courts, the statute offers us important lessons in how consumer privacy laws should work. Nearly thirty years after its passage, it continues to be feared by companies that would like to persistently harass us for their own selfish benefit. In some cases, such as in its treatment of junk fax, it has largely outlasted the technology that it was intended to cover. And, most significantly, it has managed to walk a fine line on the regulation of speech while surviving every First Amendment challenge to date (albeit with a couple of bruises).

    This book hasn't covered every nuance of the TCPA. It contains many simplifications and probably an unsupported statistic or two. Still, if you have read it up to this point, you know more about this law than 99.99999% of the American public. Now it's up to you to use the private right of action profitably but responsibly. In the Epilogue I'll talk a little bit about how this works in practice.

EPILOGUE: TAKING OUT THE TRASH

In the Prologue, I described how nuisance callers repeatedly assailed my solitude and disrupted my dinner. You're probably wondering how I dealt with them. Regrettably, I am bound by several confidentiality agreements and am unable to share my personal TCPA stories. Nor can I dispense any kind of practical legal advice, because I'm not a licensed attorney. Nonetheless, this book would be incomplete without a vague and all-too-brief description of the procedure that can be used for punishing these pests.

The sad truth is that many robocallers are difficult to identify, let alone punish. By talking to a live agent you might be able to use social engineering tricks to glean a few hints as to where an anonymous caller is located. However, those who are secretive about their identities usually place other impediments in the way of legal process. Your only recourse against them may be extralegal, and it's hard to justify a 10,000 mile trip to East Bumfuggistan just so you can firebomb a spammer's call center.

You are far more likely to collect damages from callers who make only a modest effort to remain anonymous. Many debt collectors are in this category. They sometimes use robocall messages that are missing the required identification, but there is almost always a working callback phone number or Caller ID that allows them to be easily unmasked. Political organizations and non-profit fundraisers are also usually traceable when they illegally robocall cell phones. (As you know very well by now, landline subscribers have little choice but to put up with these types of calls. Unless, of course, they fall back on the firebombing option.)

Once a robocaller has been identified and deemed sue-worthy, there is a critical decision to be made. Should you hire a lawyer or should you negotiate a settlement on your own? I've had success with the latter approach, but it isn't a good idea for everyone. I actually earned a law degree at one point, for reasons that are beyond comprehension, and that gives me a bit of an advantage when writing a demand letter. I know how to effectively employ phrases such as "cease and desist," "available statutory remedies," and "rule against perpetuities." (I have yet to use the rule against perpetuities, but I keep it ready in case anyone tries to foist an unwanted perpetuity on me.) But I also know my limits. If a case involves dozens of calls or includes possible FDCPA violations, it's best to let a professional handle it to avoid screwing it up.

Sending a certified letter to a robocaller can be very satisfying. Its arrival is usually an "oh shit" moment for the recipient. You can sign up for an email notification from the post office so you can savor it in real time. Unless you wrote your letter in crayon or misspelled "telephone," it is likely to be taken very seriously. There will soon be a call from the company's attorney, seeking to resolve the matter with a minimum of publicity, and the $8 you spent on postage will be returned to you many times over. It won't be enough money for you to quit your job and retire at age 37, but it's probably more than you can make from writing a book like this one.

These are relatively trifling claims compared to most corporate transactions, and yet the lawyers who respond to them are not the inexperienced lackeys that you might expect. One of my demand letters led to a settlement call from a partner at a prestigious firm. In another case—in which I was seeking only a symbolic $300 from a non-profit political group—I spoke with a prominent Washington attorney who had once argued before the Supreme Court. Clearly, many robocallers are wary of the potential consequences of mishandling these types of complaints. They are not going to reject a reasonable demand for compensation if there's any risk that it might otherwise turn into a multi-million dollar class action.

After negotiating a few settlements, I've observed that these corporate lawyers are exceedingly polite and rarely argumentative in this setting. They might haggle a bit over the amount that their clients will pay, but a lengthy debate isn't worth their time (at a billing rate of $400 an hour or more). The evidence of the phone calls—recordings, lists of dates and times, and photos of a cell phone with the spammer's Caller ID displayed on it—is not discussed. Both sides know that the calls were made, and both know that they were illegal.

That doesn't mean that they were the caller's fault, however. The lawyer will concede that his client must pay damages under the TCPA's strict liability rules, but will *never* admit blame. There is always some unnamed "subcontractor" who was supposed to perform a "cell phone scrub" to ensure that only landline numbers were called. It is this party's negligence that led to the violations. Please try to ignore the fact that the unsolicited robocalls would have been equally offensive if they had been made to a landline phone.

So what happens if you hire an attorney to handle your case instead of sending a letter yourself? You may get a larger settlement, or maybe even a court judgment, but will also learn an unfortunate lesson about the unfairness of the system. Income taxes are owed on the entire amount—including the portion that goes straight to legal fees and expenses without ever entering your possession. This is a consequence of the tax code modifications that were signed by President Donald Trump in 2017. (Congress proved it still has a sense of humor by referring to these changes as "tax reform.") Suppose you are in the 30% tax bracket, including both state and federal taxes, and that you have a contingency arrangement in which your lawyer keeps 40% of the payout. That $5,000 settlement now looks an awful lot like $1,500.

Attorneys' fees (and their tax implications) are less of a concern if you pursue your claim as the lead plaintiff in a class action. Even though it was never Senator Hollings' intent, the TCPA seems ready-made for this approach. The typical offender has not just bothered you with an illegal robocall or two; he has also harassed thousands of other people. Most of these victims know nothing about the statute and will never be compensated unless you fight the battle on their behalf.

Some plaintiffs' attorneys have been extraordinarily successful with TCPA class actions. Three of the big names are Jay Edelson, Todd Friedman, and Abbas Kazerounian. (Kazerounian gave the winning argument in the famous *Marks* case, but was also involved in the "Facey" debacle.) And yet, there are reasons why a class action might be unworkable. Let's look at a few:

You may not be an adequate class representative. A serious criminal conviction, a history of dishonesty, or a conflict of interest is usually enough to disqualify someone from serving as a lead plaintiff in a class action. But there's another way that a class rep can become inadequate: by dying. Litigation of this kind can take years to resolve, so don't undertake it unless you are in good health and expect to be around for the conclusion.

You might have signed an arbitration agreement. Here's an example of how this works. Suppose you sign up for service with the local cable TV provider. There will probably be some fine print in your service contract, stating that you agree to arbitrate any dispute instead of filing a lawsuit. This is mainly to protect the company from a deluge of litigation when the signal goes out at a critical time, like during the highly anticipated Labor Day weekend airing of all 44 episodes of *She's the Sheriff*. However, the arbitration clause might also apply in other scenarios, as when the company carelessly robocalls you while collecting a bill owed by another customer. Does it matter that the calls involve someone else's contract, not yours? Like everything else with the TCPA, it can be argued either way.

The class may not be ascertainable. The court needs to be able to figure out who is entitled to compensation. That can be a problem when the defendant hasn't kept adequate records. It's especially frustrating when the defense claims that it had consent to make some of the calls, but it doesn't know which ones. The caller bears the burden of demonstrating consent, so why should it get away with this crap? Yet sometimes this argument works.

Other victims may file their own class actions. Actually, they don't even need to be class actions to have an impact on your case. Some phone spammers are so prolific that they simultaneously attract numerous lawsuits from all over the country. These cases can be combined as "multi district litigation," which will usually result in your lawsuit being transferred to a judge in an inconvenient location. Is your attorney going to enjoy traveling to the District Court of Guam to argue each motion, while splitting fees with twenty other law firms?

The defendant might not have any money. At first glance, a bottom feeder debt collector that makes millions of illegal robocalls seems like a tempting target for a class action. But what if its bank accounts are empty, its office and equipment are leased, all of its employees are agency temps, and it has no ongoing enterprise value other than its ability to break the law with no consequences? Well, you can seize the underlying debts that the collector was pursuing, but maybe all of its calls were an effort to enforce one Columbia House Record Club agreement from 1992. Some teenage girl made off with twelve Boyz II Men CDs for a penny and then didn't purchase the six overpriced club selections that she was supposed to buy. The defendant was calling everyone in the United States to locate the girl or her heirs. Even if those CDs can be recovered and sold on eBay, the proceeds won't pay for the rum-and-Coke your lawyer bought at the airport in Guam.

An objector may try to spoil everything at the last minute. Some law firms like to meddle with other people's class action suits by objecting to the outcome, supposedly in the public interest. For example, they may complain that the settlement allocates too much money to attorneys' fees. Their solution is to be paid $300,000 for pointing it out.

Despite these potential pitfalls, I hope this book inspires you to seek justice when you are pestered by phone spammers. If you need to contact me for any reason (other than to ask for a refund), you can use the form on my website at https://dennisbrownbooks.wixsite.com/home. Also, please consider reading my other books: *Who Voted for the Hologram? A Gruff Guidebook to the Presidential Libraries* and *How Not to Run for Pope*. I promise they are less work than this one was.

NOTES

General References

The starting points for learning about the TCPA are the law itself (47 U.S.C. § 227) and the corresponding FCC regulations (47 C.F.R. § 1200). Just as important are the FCC's orders, decisions, and other musings about the statute. Most of these are available directly from the Commission (https://www.fcc.gov/general/telemarketing-and-robocalls) or from the TCPA's mortal enemy ACA International (https://www.acainternational.org/tcpa/tcpa-compliance-materials).

The best resources for staying up-to-date with the law are Squire Patton Boggs' TCPA World (https://tcpaworld.com) and Drinker Biddle's TCPA Blog (http://tcpablog.com). Both are defense-oriented blogs from law firms that would love to see the TCPA struck from the books so they can return to their true vocation: representing hobos who are arrested for hopping on railroad boxcars. It doesn't pay as well as defending Capital One or Wells Fargo, but it is so much more rewarding.

If you prefer your legal news to be delivered monthly rather than daily, check out Copilevitz, Lam & Raney's Telemarketing Connections Newsletter (http://clrkc.com) or Kelley Drye's TCPA Tracker (https://www.kelleydrye.com/News-Events/Publications/Newsletters/TCPA-Tracker).

Introduction

Multiple sources have confirmed that the dramatic increase in robocalls in recent years is not just our imagination. The most reliable data is probably from YouMail. The company reports that the number of robocalls in the United States jumped by 56.8% in 2018 to roughly 47.8 billion (https://www.prnewswire.com/news-releases/nearly-48-billion-robocalls-made-in-2018-according-to-youmail-robocall-index-300782638.html).

Anecdotal evidence of the problem is also alarming. A Georgia TV station recently reported on an elderly couple who receive an average of more than twenty robocalls on their landline phone each day. On one day, the tally reached forty-one by 5 PM. ("Savannah

Couple Says They Received Over 40 Robocalls in One Day" by JoAnn Merrigan, Feb. 7, 2019, WSAV-TV Savannah, https://www.wsav.com/recalls/consumer-recall-reports/robocalls-the-story-of-one-savannah-couple/1763353842) What the story did not mention is that many of these calls were probably legal, since landline users are fair game under the FCC's interpretation of the TCPA.

For a sampling of recipients' reaction to robocalls, see "'Nuts! Out of Control. Do Something!': American Robocall Outrage" by Allan Smith, NBC News, May 27, 2019 (https://www.nbcnews.com/politics/congress/nuts-out-control-do-something-american-robocall-outrage-n1009351). A typical consumer complaint to the FCC: "Someone should shoot these assholes."

Lawsuit statistics are from WebRecon, which reports an average of more than 4,000 TCPA suits each year between 2015 and 2018 (https://webrecon.com/webrecon-stats-for-dec-2018-2018-ends-with-a-whimper).

Wilma Donkins declined to be interviewed for this book, and threatened to sic her dachshund on the author if he shows up at her door.

There have been several "how-to-sue" manuals written for non-lawyers to collect damages under the TCPA. You can even buy a kit for $47 that contains demand letter templates and instructions for their use. Most of these materials have not been reviewed by the author. When evaluating them, you are advised to steer clear of books that recommend suing telemarketers in small claims court. This was a good strategy in 1998, but now most TCPA claims are resolved either in pre-litigation discussions or in federal court. Also, the easiest cases to pursue usually do not involve telemarketers.

Prologue: Attack of the Trash Calls

"Darnell" is a pseudonym for a specific individual who was referenced in some of the vexatious calls that the author received. "XYZ Receivables" is a fictitious name. The other names and initials referenced in this section belong to actual entities who behaved in the manner that is described.

1. Ernest Writes a Law

The "IQ test" quote, and many other great lines from Ernest Hollings, can be found in "Did You Hear: 38 Classic 'Hollingsisms'," *Times and Democrat* (Orangeburg, S.C.), Dec. 16, 2004 (https://thetandd.com/news/did-you-hear-classic-hollings-isms/article_8327afa8-b598-5930-aeb0-3a09e6d688e4.html).

Tipper Gore's "curling my hair" quote is from "Parents Vs. Rock" by Roger Wolmuth, *People*, Sep. 16, 1985 (https://people.com/archive/cover-story-parents-vs-rock-vol-23-no-12).

The infamous Senate record labeling hearing of Sep. 19, 1985 can be viewed on YouTube. (Dee Snider's testimony at https://www.youtube.com/watch?v=S0Vyr1TylTE)

The George Carlin case is F.C.C. v. Pacifica Foundation, 438 U.S. 726 (1978). The "Porn Wars" track is on *Frank Zappa Meets the Mothers of Prevention* (1985).

The letter from the *Union and Advertiser* was reproduced in the *Telephony* journal on Feb. 20, 1909, under the heading "Housekeeper Objects to Telephone Advertising." An even earlier reference to telemarketing appeared in *Western Electrician* on Sep. 12, 1903. Some of these historical sources have been collected by Thomas H. White as part of his "United States Early Radio History" series (https://earlyradiohistory.us/sec003.htm).

The history of telemarketing, including Murray Roman's role in it, is discussed in "Have We Reached the Party to Whom We Are Speaking?" by Don Oldenburg, *Washington Post*, Oct. 20, 2002 (https://www.washingtonpost.com/archive/lifestyle/2002/10/20/have-we-reached-the-party-to-whom-we-are-speaking/19eb8ffc-83ac-461e-be6e-a83f27aa5fc8). An index card deck from Roman's Campaign Communications Institute of America (dated Mar. 1980) is available in Carnegie Mellon University's digital archives (http://digitalcollections.library.cmu.edu/awweb/awarchive?type=file&item=689055). Roman was eulogized in the *New York Times* on May 9, 1984 (https://www.nytimes.com/1984/05/09/obituaries/murray-roman-head-of-marketing-concern.html).

The injured child incident was referenced in "'Junk' Phone Calls: Danger on the Line?" by James Barron, *New York Times*, May

21, 1988 (https://www.nytimes.com/1988/05/21/style/consumer-s-world-junk-phone-calls-danger-on-the-line.html). The Hawaiian vacation robocall was described in "Curbing the Telephone Robots" by Edmund L. Andrews, *New York Times*, Oct. 30, 1991 (https://www.nytimes.com/1991/10/30/business/curbing-the-telephone-robots.html). The latter article also marked the first national attention for Kathryn Moser and her AAA-1 Lucky Leprechaun chimney sweeping service.

The legislative history of the TCPA is mostly taken from the *Congressional Record*, since *Tiger Beat* and *TV Guide* didn't cover much of the debate. Shah Legal Representation's "TCPA Defense Library" has a web page that helpfully includes most of the relevant materials (http://www.tcpadefense.com/legislative-history).

President George H.W. Bush's signing statement is available from "The American Presidency Project" at University of California Santa Barbara (https://www.presidency.ucsb.edu/documents/statement-signing-the-telephone-consumer-protection-act-1991).

2. The TCPA: Trespassing Callers Punished Appropriately

Most of this chapter is based on the language of the TCPA and its accompanying regulations, and on the FCC's TCPA report and order that was released on Oct. 16, 1992. There's not much more to say about it than that.

3. The Courts Have Their Say

Here are the case citations, not guaranteed to be in precise Bluebook form:

- Central Hudson Gas & Elec. Corp. v. Public Service Comm'n, 447 U.S. 557 (1980)

- Moser v. F.C.C., 46 F.3d 970 (9th Cir. 1995), *rev'g* 826 F. Supp. 360 (D. Or. 1993), *cert. denied*, 515 U.S. 1161 (1995)

- Destination Ventures, Ltd. v. F.C.C., 46 F.3d 54 (9th Cir. 1995), *aff'g* 844 F. Supp. 632 (D. Or. 1994)

- Missouri ex rel. Nixon v. American Blast Fax, Inc., 323 F.3d 649 (8th Cir. 2003), *rev'g* 196 F. Supp. 2d 920 (E.D. Mo. 2002)

- Interactive Digital Software Ass'n v. St. Louis County, Mo., 200 F. Supp. 2d 1126 (E.D. Mo. 2002), *rev'd by* 329 F.3d 954 (8th Cir. 2003)

- Mims v. Arrow Financial Services, LLC, 565 U.S. 368 (2012)

4. The Crackdown of 2003

For background on Do-Not-Call laws, see "Do Not Call: The History of Do Not Call and How Telemarketing Has Evolved," National Association of Attorneys General, *NAGTRI Journal*, Aug. 2016 (https://www.naag.org/publications/nagtri-journal/volume-1-number-4/do-not-call-the-history-of-do-not-call-and-how-telemarketing-has-evolved.php).

President George W. Bush's statement on the Do-Not-Call list was issued on June 27, 2003 (https://georgewbush-whitehouse.archives.gov/news/releases/2003/06/text/20030627-3.html).

The initial case that delayed the Do-Not-Call list was U.S. Security v. F.T.C., 282 F. Supp. 2d 1285 (W.D. Okla. 2003). It was followed by Mainstream Marketing Services, Inc. v. F.T.C., 345 F.3d 850 (10th Cir. 2003), *rev'g* 283 F. Supp. 2d 1151 (D. Colo. 2003), *aff'd by* 358 F.3d 1228 (10th Cir. 2004).

AT&T's work on the Do-Not-Call project is celebrated in "Project Management and the Do Not Call Registry: The Government's Big IT Success" by Alice Dragoon, *CIO*, June 1, 2004 (https://www.cio.com/article/2439625/project-management-and-the-do-not-call-registry--the-government-s-big-it-success.html).

The FCC's Notice of Apparent Liability against AT&T was released on Nov. 3, 2003 (https://transition.fcc.gov/eb/Orders/2003/FCC-03-267A1.html) and was resolved via consent decree on July 9, 2004 (https://transition.fcc.gov/eb/Orders/2004/FCC-04-169A1.html).

The FTC's Telemarketing Sales Rule (TSR) is at 16 C.F.R. § 310. The FCC's predictive dialer rules and Chairman Powell's statement were from its TCPA report and order of July 3, 2003 (https://www.fcc.gov/general/telemarketing-and-robocalls).

Statistics on cell phone usage are from "Atlanta Is Top Cell Phone User," CNN, Oct. 15, 2003 (https://money.cnn.com/2003/10/14/technology/cell_phones/index.htm).

The wireless portability database was originally operated by Neustar. Today it is managed by iconectiv (https://iconectiv.com/NPAC).

5. Political Robocalls: One More Reason Not to Vote

For a look at how some people are using political robocalls today, see "Suspected Racist CD Distributor Appears to Be Responsible for Robocalls in California" by Ben Olson & Cameron Rasmusson, *Sandpoint Reader* (Idaho), May 24, 2018 (http://sandpointreader.com/suspected-racist-cd-distributor-appears-responsible-robocalls-california).

As this book goes to press, some states *still* haven't realized that telemarketing laws can't single out political speech for restrictions that don't apply to other types of calls. Montana's defective law was recently struck down in Victory Processing, LLC v. Fox, No. 18-35163, 2019 WL 4264718 (9th Cir. Sept. 10, 2019).

The Texas foul-up was exposed in "Lawmakers Could Face Fines over 'Robocalls' to Cell Phones" by Tim Eaton, *Austin American-Statesman*, Jan. 23, 2010.

The Navy text message case is Campbell-Ewald Co. v. Gomez, 577 U.S. ___, 136 S. Ct. 663 (2016). Stephen King's publisher was rebuked in Satterfield v. Simon & Schuster, Inc., 569 F.3d 946 (9th Cir. 2009).

For discussion of the various dirty tricks, see:

- "Investigation of Kleeb Phone Calls Closed" by Zach Pluhacek, *Lincoln Journal Star*, June 5, 2007 (https://journalstar.com/news/local/govt-and-politics/investigation-of-kleeb-phone-calls-closed/article_eb09c970-6f11-55e9-a591-efaee2d8ccaf.html)

- "Political Robo-Calls Have New Twist: Fake Caller ID" by Jake Wagman, *St. Louis Post-Dispatch*, Nov. 24, 2010 (https://www.stltoday.com/news/local/govt-and-politics/political-robo-calls-have-new-twist-fake-caller-id/article_090c7b39-32f2-51d8-80e4-e16ea1b1d886.html)

- Oklahoma ex rel. Edmonson v. Pope, 505 F. Supp. 2d 1098 (W.D. Okla. 2007)

- Maryland v. Universal Elections, 787 F. Supp. 2d 408 (D. Md. 2011)

- "Man Behind Robocall Scandal Speaks Exclusively to WJZ," WJZ-TV Baltimore, June 12, 2012 (https://baltimore.cbslocal.com/2012/06/12/man-behind-robocall-scandal-speaks-exclusively-to-wjz)

- "Julius Henson Will Spend 60 Days in Jail for Robocalls Case," WJZ-TV Baltimore, June 13, 2012 (https://baltimore.cbslocal.com/2012/06/13/julius-henson-faces-sentencing-in-robocalls-case)

For a look at how some political campaigns are circumventing the TCPA's autodialer restrictions by sending text spam with peer-to-peer messaging apps, see "Why You May Be Getting Unsolicited Text Messages from Trump, Other Political Candidates" by Vic Ryckaert, *Indianapolis Star*, Oct. 26, 2018 (https://www.indystar.com/story/news/politics/2018/10/26/texts-trump-why-you-may-getting-texts-voting/1749084002).

6. Long Distance Panhandlers

The three big Supreme Court cases were:

- Schaumburg v. Citizens for a Better Environment, 444 U.S. 620 (1980)

- Sec'y of State of Maryland v. Joseph H. Munson Co., Inc., 467 U.S. 947 (1984)

- Riley v. Nat'l Fed'n of the Blind of North Carolina, 487 U.S. 781 (1988)

Errol Copilevitz was profiled in "Let It Ring: When the Phone Rings and a Dubious Charity Asks for Money, You Can Thank Free-Speech Lawyer Errol Copilevitz for the Call" by Kris Hundley & Kendall Taggart, *Tampa Bay Times* & Center for Investigative Reporting, Sep. 12, 2013 (https://www.tampabay.com/news/let-it-ring-errol-copilevitz-and-americas-worst-charities/2141401). Also see "America's 50 Worst Charities Rake in Nearly $1 Billion for Corporate Fundraisers" by the same authors, June 6, 2013 (https://www.tampabay.com/news/nation/americas-50-worst-charities-rake-in-nearly-1-billion-for-corporate/2339540).

The FTC's victory in Soundboard Ass'n v. F.T.C., 888 F.3d 1261 (D.C. Cir. 2018) affirmed that the TSR does not allow soundboard calls to be made for telemarketing purposes. However, a couple of marketers are now trying to get the FCC to carve out an exemption to the TCPA for these same types of calls. ("New Petition Seeking FCC Clarification That Calls Using Soundboard Technology Are Not 'Entirely Prerecorded Calls' Prohibited by the TCPA" by Laura H. Phillips & Qiusi Y. Newcom, TCPA Blog, Sep. 20, 2019. http://tcpablog.com/new-petition-seeking-fcc-clarification-that-calls-using-soundboard-technology) The companies argue that the TCPA should apply only to *non-interactive* robocalls that are *entirely* prerecorded. This is probably the most quixotic TCPA argument that has been attempted since Celshare's automatic dialer petition of 1992. Is the FCC going to read a couple of extra adjectives into the statute—inviting anger from the public and another slap-down by the courts—just to make it easier for telemarketers to get away with violating the FTC's rules? The commissioners are more likely to let radio stations announce George Carlin's seven dirty words instead of their legal call signs at the top of every hour.

7. Debt Collectors: The World Champions of Robocalling

For an interesting and informative overview of the debt collection industry, see *Bad Paper: Chasing Debt from Wall Street to the Underworld* by Jake Halpern (2014).

The FDCPA is codified at 15 U.S.C. § 1692.

The FTC's complaint against GC Services was filed on Feb. 14, 2017 (https://www.ftc.gov/enforcement/cases-proceedings/gc-services-limited-partnership).

The FTC announced its settlement with Allied Interstate on Oct. 21, 2010 (https://www.ftc.gov/news-events/press-releases/2010/10/debt-collector-will-pay-175-million-settle-ftc-charges). The Los Angeles County District Attorney's office announced its settlement on Oct. 31, 2018 (http://da.lacounty.gov/media/news/debt-collection-company-agrees-9-million-settlement-over-illegal-phone-calling-practices). The law office of Luftman, Heck & Associates LLP observes that "Allied Interstate has had a great number of legal actions filed against them arising from unfair and deceptive collection practices." (https://www.ohiodebthelp.com/debt-collections/collection-agencies/allied-interstate) It cites cases brought by the states of Ohio, Maryland, Minnesota, and Oregon.

Statistics on FDCPA lawsuits are once again from WebRecon (https://webrecon.com/webrecon-stats-for-dec-2018-2018-ends-with-a-whimper). The average from 2015 to 2018 is just over 10,000 per year.

For insight into skip tracing techniques, see "Ron Brown, Skip Tracer, Talks Debt Collecting" by Jay MacDonald, CreditCards.com, Aug. 3, 2012 (https://www.creditcards.com/credit-card-news/skip-tracer-debt-collection-ron-brown-interview-1272.php).

James Watson's big win was Watson v. NCO Group, 462 F. Supp. 2d 641 (E.D. Pa. 2006). The Santinos' unfortunate loss was Santino v. NCO Financial Systems, Inc., No. 09-CV-982-JTC (W.D.N.Y. Feb. 24, 2011). The *Chevron* deference doctrine comes from Chevron U.S.A., Inc. v. National Resources Defense Council, Inc., 467 U.S. 837 (1984). Now that courts seem to be moving toward an anti-deference stance, as with the *ACA Int'l* decision discussed in Chapter 10, it may be time for another challenge to the FCC's 1992 loophole.

The *Seinfeld* reference is from "The Red Dot" episode in Season 3. George's response to his boss: "Was that wrong? Should I not have done that? I tell ya, I gotta plead ignorance on this thing, because if anyone had said anything to me at all when I first started here that sort of thing was frowned upon...."

For an example of a court reaching a clearly incorrect verdict in a debt collection TCPA case, see Roy v. Dell Fin. Services, LLC, No. 3:13-cv-738, 2013 WL 3678551 (M.D. Pa. July 12, 2013). The complaint involved a creditor who robocalled a debtor on his office phone, which was a 1-800 line that incurs a charge for each call. Roughly 1,000 illegal calls were alleged. The district judge thought that the FCC's TCPA loophole for residential landlines also protects debt collectors in all cases, even when calling cell numbers and other types of phone lines that result in a charge to the recipient. Fortunately, the plaintiff appealed this erroneous ruling and the defendant agreed to settle.

The Case of the $147,000 Jury Verdict was First Nat'l Collection Bureau v. Walker, 348 S.W.3d 329 (Tex. App. 2011). The Case of the Unpaid X-Ray Bill was Mais v. Gulf Coast Collection Bureau, Inc., 768 F.3d 1110 (11th Cir. 2014), *rev'g* 944 F. Supp. 2d 1226 (S.D. Fla. 2013).

8. Turning Robocalls (and Faxes) into Riches

The crushing verdict against Gene Kalsky was upheld in Gen-Kal Pipe & Steel Corp. v. M. S. Wholesale Plumbing, Inc., 2019 Ark. App. 117 (Ark. Ct. App. 2019). The New Jersey courts considered the seizure of Kalsky's home and personal property in M. S. Wholesale Plumbing, Inc. v. Gen-Kal Pipe & Steel Corp., No. A-2502-17T2 (N.J. Super. Ct. App. Div. Jan. 15, 2019). For an example of media coverage of this tear-jerking saga, see "1 Fax + 1 Lawsuit = $12.5M Award" by Bill Barlow, *Cape May County Herald*, Jul. 23, 2018 (https://www.capemaycountyherald.com/news/article_476ec758-8eb1-11e8-9587-bb968a9fa7e4.html).

For a less sympathetic view of Gen-Kal's fax advertising habits, see this review by Rick Myrick of Michigan on Yelp and Facebook.

It was posted on June 30, 2016 while the lawsuit was already well underway:

> "If this company's products are as good as their service, stay the hell away.
>
> "Their fax machine has been calling my home number for the last 6 months. Most of the time between 2 and 3 AM!!! I have left them numerous messages and they have yet to remove my number from their call list."
>
> (https://www.yelp.com/biz/gen-kal-pipe-and-steel-mount-laurel and https://www.facebook.com/pages/Gen-Kal-Pipe-Steel-Corp/121844547872603)

The Solicited Fax Rule was overturned in Bais Yaakov of Spring Valley v. F.C.C., 852 F.3d 1078 (D.C. Cir. 2017).

The Lakers won a temporary victory over Facey's beau in Emanuel v. The Los Angeles Lakers, Inc., No. CV 12-9936-GW(SHx), 2013 WL 1719035 (C.D. Cal. Apr. 18, 2013), only to ultimately settle the case while it was under appeal. Then they lost their insurance claim for the resulting costs in Los Angeles Lakers, Inc. v. Federal Insurance Company, 869 F.3d 795 (9th Cir. 2017). With the way the team's fortunes have declined since the texting debacle, it's surprising that its attorney didn't also fall and break his suing shoulder in a snowboarding accident.

The case that is mandatory reading is Soppet v. Enhanced Recovery Co., LLC, 679 F.3d 637 (7th Cir. 2012). The case that brought Article III defenses to the forefront is Spokeo v. Robins, 578 U.S. ___, 136 S. Ct. 1540 (2016). And the case that established that shoeboxes full of phones don't have legal rights is Stoops v. Wells Fargo Bank, N.A., 197 F. Supp. 3d 782 (W.D. Pa. 2016).

A strong argument for Article III standing for recipients of robocalls is found at Mey v. Got Warranty, Inc., 193 F. Supp. 3d 641 at 644-45 (N.D. W. Va. 2016):

> "For consumers with prepaid cell phones or limited-minute plans, unwanted calls cause direct, concrete, monetary injury by depleting limited minutes that the consumer has paid for or by causing the consumer to incur charges for calls. In addition, all ATDS calls deplete a cell phone's battery, and the cost of

electricity to recharge the phone is also a tangible harm. While certainly small, the cost is real, and the cumulative effect could be consequential.

"Of more import, such calls also cause intangible injuries, regardless of whether the consumer has a prepaid cell phone or a plan with a limited number of minutes. The main types of intangible harm that unlawful calls cause are (1) invasion of privacy, (2) intrusion upon and occupation of the capacity of the consumer's cell phone, and (3) wasting the consumer's time or causing the risk of personal injury due to interruption and distraction."

The plight of the Florida woman who reported 6,000 calls from Wells Fargo is reported at "Cashing in on Illegal Robo Calls to Your Cell" by Jackie Callaway, WFTX-TV Fort Myers, Nov. 19, 2015 (https://www.fox4now.com/money/consumer/woman-sues-wells-fargo-bank-after-robo-dialer-called-her-cell-phone-over-6000-times). Her case was settled in mediation. See Bourgeois v. Wells Fargo Bank, N.A., No. 3:15-cv-00302-MCR-EMT Doc. 36 (N.D. Fla. Nov. 18, 2015).

The initial three-part *Forbes* "Phoney Lawsuits" series by John O'Brien is from Mar. 14, 2017 (starts at https://www.forbes.com/sites/legalnewsline/2017/03/14/phoney-lawsuits-a-federal-law-is-giving-litigious-people-a-new-income-stream). O'Brien has continued to write additional articles assailing TCPA plaintiffs.

An example of a case in which Philip Charvat used Ohio's Consumer Sales Protection Act to enforce a technical TCPA violation is Charvat v. Telelytics, LLC, 2006 Ohio 4623 (Ohio Ct. App. 2006). The "veteran litigant" quote is from Charvat v. National Holdings Corp., No. 2:14-cv-2205 Doc. 32 (S.D. Ohio May 26, 2015).

The ruling in the 222-2222 case is Konopca v. FDS Bank, No. 15-cv-01547 (PGS) (D.N.J. Nov. 22, 2017).

For another example of a questionable case, see Viggiano v. Kohl's Department Stores, Inc., No. 17-0243-BRM-TJB, 2017 U.S. Dist. LEXIS 193999 (D.N.J. Nov. 27, 2017). The plaintiff signed up to receive text message advertisements from a store, and was instructed to text "STOP", "CANCEL", "QUIT",

"UNSUBSCRIBE", or "END" if she wanted to unsubscribe. She instead texted "I've changed my mind and don't want to receive these anymore." When that didn't work, she tried "Please do not send any further messages." Finally, she sent "I don't want these messages anymore! This is your last warning!" The store once again ignored her request, resulting in a $100 million class action claim. The judge was not impressed by the plaintiff's texting verbosity, however, and ruled that her attempts to revoke consent were unreasonable.

9. The Scam-Based Economy

Sources for this chapter include Genesis 25-28 by God (c. 5th Century BCE), the song "One Piece at a Time" by Wayne Kemp (recorded by Johnny Cash c. 1976 CE), and "The Secret History of McDonald's Filet-O-Fish" by Áine Cain, *Business Insider*, Mar. 6, 2019 (https://www.businessinsider.com/history-of-mcdonalds-filet-o-fish-2018-1). An eclectic bunch indeed.

References for the Ken Taves case include:

- "Bank Sold Credit Card Data to Felon" by Jeff Leeds, *Los Angeles Times*, Sep. 11, 1999 (https://www.latimes.com/archives/la-xpm-1999-sep-11-mn-8867-story.html)

- "Web Gumshoe Runs Credit Card Scam to Ground" by Mike Brunker, NBC News, Sep. 23, 1999 (http://www.nbcnews.com/id/3078814)

- Dr. John Faughnan's personal website (https://www.faughnan.com/ccfraud.html)

- Robb Evans & Associates LLC's website discussing receivership activities in attempting to recover the stolen money (https://www.robbevans.com/find-a-case/j-k-publications-inc-et-al-receiver)

References on Rachel and related scams include:

- FCC citation of Cardholder Services, Inc., Mar. 2, 2007 (https://transition.fcc.gov/eb/Orders/2007/DA-07-977A1.html). The company's incorporation information is available from the California Secretary of State's office, with the last statement filed on May 22, 1991 (https://businessfilings.sos.ca.gov/frmDetail.asp?CorpID=01681863).

- Various FTC cases (https://www.ftc.gov/enforcement/cases-proceedings), such as the complaint against Castle Rock Capital Management, Inc. and Roy M. Cox, Jr., Dec. 19, 2011 (https://www.ftc.gov/enforcement/cases-proceedings/092-3193/castle-rock-capital-management-inc)

- Various internet complaint sites, including ComplaintWire c. 2012-2014 (https://complaintwire.org/complaint/QJYBAAAAAAA/cardholders-services/9)

- "The Hunt for Rachel at Cardholder Services" by Michael Jones, four-part post at On the Spot Blog, begins May 24, 2012 (http://onthespotblog.com/the-hunt-for-rachel-at-cardholder-services)

References on the car warranty scams include:

- "Tracking Down Auto Warranty Callers" by Azadeh Ensha, *New York Times* "Wheels" blog, May 12, 2009 (https://wheels.blogs.nytimes.com/2009/05/12/tracking-down-auto-warranty-callers)

- "2 Executives Admit Auto-Service Telemarketing Scam," Associated Press via Fox News, Dec. 13, 2010 (https://www.foxnews.com/us/2-executives-admit-auto-service-telemarketing-scam)

- Statements on Transcontinental Warranty case, U.S. Attorney's Office for the Southern District of Illinois, 2010-

2011 (https://www.justice.gov/usao-sdil/victim-witness-assistance/transcontinental-warranty)

- "St. Louis Area Mansion Remains Money-Losing Legacy for US Fidelis" by Matthew Hathaway, *Waterloo-Cedar Falls Courier*, Nov. 19, 2010 (https://wcfcourier.com/business/local/st-louis-area-mansion-remains-money-losing-legacy-for-us/article_9637b38c-f3cc-11df-bb2f-001cc4c002e0.html)

- "Former Owner of US Fidelis Pleads Guilty to State Charges" by Rachel Lippmann, St. Louis Public Radio, Apr. 5, 2012 (https://news.stlpublicradio.org/post/former-owner-us-fidelis-pleads-guilty-state-charges)

- Statement on sentencing of Darain Atkinson, U.S. Attorney's Office for the Eastern District of Missouri, Sep. 25, 2012 (https://archives.fbi.gov/archives/stlouis/press-releases/2012/final-u.s.-fidelis-co-owner-sentenced-on-conspiracy-and-tax-fraud-charges)

- "A Look at US Fidelis from the Inside" by Toni McQuilken, P&A (Providers & Administrators), Sep. 30, 2013 (https://www.providers-administrators.com/346892/a-look-at-us-fidelis-from-the-inside)

- "Spoils of US Fidelis," Sometimes Interesting blog post about Darain Atkinson's mansion, Apr. 15, 2015 (https://sometimes-interesting.com/2015/04/15/spoils-of-us-fidelis)

The FTC's action against the Reynolds cancer "charities" was announced on May 19, 2015 (https://www.ftc.gov/news-events/press-releases/2015/05/ftc-all-50-states-dc-charge-four-cancer-charities-bilking-over). The failed TCPA case against them was Spiegel v. Reynolds, No. 1:15-cv-08504, 2017 WL 4535951 (N.D. Ill. Oct. 11, 2017). One of ACS' other controversial endeavors was discussed in "State of Minnesota Suing Fundraiser for Veterans' Charity" by Mark Brunswick, *Minneapolis Star*

Tribune, May 25, 2016 (http://www.startribune.com/state-is-suing-fundraiser-for-veterans-charity/380828281). The disposition of this case was included in the FTC's "Donate with Honor" report of July 19, 2018 (https://www.ftc.gov/system/files/attachments/press-releases/ftc-states-combat-fraudulent-charities-falsely-claim-help-veterans-servicemembers/dwh_list-enforcement-actions_1.pdf).

The FCC has issued Truth in Caller ID forfeitures against:

- Steven Blumenstock, Jan. 13, 2017 (https://transition.fcc.gov/eb/Orders/2017/DA-17-57A1.html)

- Adrian Abramovich, et al., May 10, 2018 (https://transition.fcc.gov/eb/Orders/2018/FCC-18-58A1.html). Includes the statements from Chairman Pai and Commissioner Rosenworcel.

- Best Insurance Contracts, Inc. and Philip Roesel d/b/a Wilmington Insurance Quotes, Sep. 26, 2018 (https://transition.fcc.gov/eb/Orders/2018/FCC-18-134A1.html)

- Affordable Enterprises of Arizona, LLC, Sep. 26, 2018 (https://transition.fcc.gov/eb/Orders/2018/FCC-18-135A1.html)

The Abramovich case is discussed in "Miami Man Made Nearly 100 Million Robocalls. Now He's Paying a Big Price." by Rob Wile, *Miami Herald*, May 11, 2018 (https://www.miamiherald.com/news/local/community/miami-dade/article210861109.html). TripAdvisor's investigation is described in "On the Trail of the Robocall King" by Alex W. Palmer, *Wired*, Mar. 25, 2019 (https://www.wired.com/story/on-the-trail-of-the-robocall-king). Portions of Abramovich's Senate testimony are available on YouTube, and the image is a screenshot from this hearing (questioning by Sen. Markey at https://www.youtube.com/watch?v=j35fRAT2ChI).

A side note on the Truth in Caller ID Act: it only applies to callers who intend to "defraud, cause harm, or wrongfully obtain anything of value." However, it contains an exemption for "any authorized activity of a law enforcement agency." Why do law enforcement agencies need to be able to intentionally harm or defraud people or wrongfully take things? Scary stuff indeed.

10. Confusion All Around

The House hearing on MICA can be viewed on YouTube (https://www.youtube.com/watch?v=IdMKIJzZj9E). For details on Rep. Terry's fate, see "Lee Terry Find Private Life Pays Better" by Joseph Morton, *Omaha World-Herald*, July 2, 2015 (https://www.omaha.com/news/politics/lee-terry-finds-private-life-pays-better-move-to-lobbying/article_b73bca4c-b53c-5ab9-ae29-c88b17e66509.html).

For an example of how corporations argue against alleged "abuse" of the TCPA, see the "TCPA Litigation Sprawl" report by Becca Wahlquist, prepared for the U.S. Chamber Institute for Legal Reform in Aug. 2017 (https://www.instituteforlegalreform.com/uploads/sites/1/TCPA_Paper_Final.pdf).

As this book goes to press, plaintiffs are winning every ringless voicemail verdict. See "Three Strikes: Are Ringless Voicemail Providers Now 'Out' Under the TCPA?" by Eric J. Troutman, TCPA World blog, June 25, 2019 (https://tcpaworld.com/2019/06/25/three-strikes-are-ringless-voicemail-users-now-out-under-the-tcpa).

However, the Saunders v. Dyck O'Neal, Inc. case continues to be litigated in the Eastern District of Michigan. The co-inventor of the VoApps DirectDROP Voicemail system, David A. King, has weighed in with an explanation of the technology in an effort to convince the court to rule that it is not subject to the TCPA. There is no word on whether the estate of Rube Goldberg (1883-1970) will also file an amicus brief.

The VoApps system is covered (along with signaling applications that might actually be useful) by U.S. Patent No. 2012/0307647 A1, which expires on May 7, 2032 (https://patents.google.com/patent/US20120307647A1). The other technique for ringless voicemail, which uses two autodialed calls for each message, was invented by Toufic Boutros Mobarak and Ashou Han. U.S. Patent No. 8,605,869 is owned by Mobilesphere, Ltd. and expires on Oct. 5, 2031 (https://patents.google.com/patent/US8605869).

The citations for the autodialer cases are:

- ACA Int'l v. F.C.C., 885 F.3d 687 (D.C. Cir. 2018)

- Pinkus v. Sirius XM Radio, Inc., No. 16 C 10858, 2018 WL 3586186 (N.D. Ill. July 26, 2018)

- Marks v. Crunch San Diego, LLC, 904 F.3d 1041 (9th Cir. 2018)

The autodialer controversy continues to rage as an important text spam case, Gadelhak v. AT&T Services, Inc., is pending before the 7th Circuit Court of Appeals. At oral argument on Sep. 27, 2019, the parties sparred over the grammatical interpretation of the ATDS definition. The plaintiff's attorney Tim Sostrin used an interesting analogy to show that "using a random or sequential number generator" does not modify the word "store":

> "If I tell you that baseball is a sport where the players throw or hit a ball using a bat, you know that 'using a bat' does not modify 'throw.' ... It just doesn't make sense to use a generator to store numbers, one, and two, it's going to render 'store' superfluous."

For the opposite point of view, see "'Boil or Dice the Potatoes, Using a Knife'..." by Eric J. Troutman, TCPA World blog, Sep. 24, 2019 (https://tcpaworld.com/2019/09/24/boil-or-dice-the-potatoes-using-a-knife-why-the-fate-of-the-tcpas-atds-definition-may-hang-on-a-comma-obscure-rules-of-grammar-and-one-bad-analog).

A win for the defendant in *Gadelhak* would set up a circuit split with the 9th Circuit and a possible showdown in the Supreme Court. It would also make the autodialer rule largely unenforceable in part of the country, including the TCPA litigation hotbed of Chicago. Spammers would be able to send automatically dialed calls or texts to literally millions of people without even a hint of consent or a prior relationship, as long as they claimed to be working from a list of some kind. (Prerecorded voice calls to cell phones would still be illegal.) The FCC could avert this by simply reaffirming its 2003 and 2008 dialer rulings without the troubling statements it added in 2015, but it is apparently waiting on Congress to resolve the problem. Good luck with that.

One of the cases that limits a consumer's right to revoke consent is Reyes v. Lincoln Automotive Financial Services, 861 F.3d 51 (2d Cir. 2017).

Commissioner Pai's vivid "dog's breakfast" quote is from his statement of Aug. 11, 2016 (https://docs.fcc.gov/public/attachments/FCC-16-99A5.pdf).

The federal debt collection exemption was struck down in Am. Ass'n of Political Consultants, Inc. v. F.C.C., 923 F.3d 159 (4th Cir. 2019) and Duguid v. Facebook, Inc., No. 17-15320 (9th Cir. June 13, 2019). Senators Ed Markey and Mike Lee, along with Rep. Anna Eshoo, have sponsored the Help Americans Never Get Unwanted Phone Calls (HANGUP) Act. This law would specify that federal contractors are fully subject to the TCPA, thereby repealing the exemption and saving the other circuits from having to waste their time issuing similar rulings. Despite being non-controversial and having bipartisan support, the HANGUP Act is taking an absurd amount of time to get through committee. Markey first introduced the proposal in November 2015, and it is still pending as of October 2019.

11. The Crisis Enters Its 4th Decade

The Tufts University incident was reported in "Robocalls Are Overwhelming Hospitals and Patients, Threatening a New Kind of Health Crisis" by Tony Romm, *Washington Post*, June 17, 2019 (https://www.washingtonpost.com/technology/2019/06/17/robocalls-are-overwhelming-hospitals-patients-threatening-new-kind-health-crisis). The hand surgeon's missed call is described in "It's Not Just You—Robocalls Are Becoming More Frequent" by Tara Siegel Bernard, *New York Times*, May 6, 2018 (https://www.nytimes.com/2018/05/06/your-money/robocalls-rise-illegal.html).

Other references detail the current disastrous state of TCPA enforcement:

- "How Robo-Call Moguls Outwitted the Government and Completely Wrecked the Do Not Call List" by Simon Van Zuylen-Wood, *Washington Post*, Jan. 9, 2018 (https://www.washingtonpost.com/lifestyle/magazine/how-robo-call-moguls-outwitted-the-government-and-completely-wrecked-the-do-not-call-list/2018/01/09/52c769b6-df7a-11e7-bbd0-9dfb2e37492a_story.html)

- "The FCC Has Fined Robocallers $208 Million. It's Collected $6,790." by Sarah Krouse, *Wall Street Journal*, Mar. 28, 2019 (https://www.wsj.com/articles/the-fcc-has-fined-robocallers-208-million-its-collected-6-790-11553770803)

- "The Robocall Crisis Will Never Be Totally Fixed" by Lily Hay Newman, Wired, Apr. 7, 2019 (https://www.wired.com/story/robocalls-spam-fix-stir-shaken)

- "'Do I Know You?' and Other Spam Phone Calls We Can't Get Rid Of" by Yuki Noguchi, National Public Radio, June 6, 2019 (https://www.npr.org/2019/06/06/727711432/do-i-know-you-and-other-spam-phone-calls-we-can-t-get-rid-of)

- "Scam Robocalls Are Even Fooling Hospitals. Here's How Congress Can Make That Can Stop." [sic] by Rep. Frank Pallone Jr., Rep. Greg Walden, and Dave Summitt, for NBC News, July 31, 2019 (https://www.nbcnews.com/think/opinion/scam-robocalls-are-even-fooling-hospitals-here-s-how-congress-ncna1037391)

The statement by Commissioner Starks was part of the FCC's robocall blocking order of June 7, 2019 (https://www.fcc.gov/document/fcc-affirms-robocall-blocking-default-protect-consumers-0).

The FTC announced the first "Robocall Challenge" winners on April 2, 2013 (https://www.ftc.gov/news-events/press-releases/2013/04/ftc-announces-robocall-challenge-winners).

Rep. Biggs' statement about SBRA was issued through his spokesman Daniel Stefanski. See "Biggs 1 of Only 3 Votes Against Anti-Robocall Bill" by Jeremy Duda, *AZ Mirror*, July 25, 2019 (https://www.azmirror.com/blog/biggs-1-of-only-3-votes-against-anti-robocall-bill).

Consumers' changing communication habits, and their effect on the debt collection industry, were noted in "Real Issue for Debt Collectors Is the Irrelevance of Telephones" by Ohad Samet, *American Banker*, Feb. 9, 2017 (https://www.americanbanker.com/opinion/real-issue-for-debt-collectors-is-the-irrelevance-of-telephones). Samet points out that the debates over the TCPA and FDCPA are focused on "a disappearing world" of "phone calls and written letters" that are "inconsistent with a new generation of borrowers that responds to emails and social media posts."

Epilogue: Taking Out the Trash

You're still here? It's a nice day, you really need to get outside and stop reading this stuff.

APPENDIX: THE TELEPHONE CONSUMER PROTECTION ACT

Findings
Public Law 102-243, Dec. 20, 1991 (105 Stat. 2394-95)

The Congress finds that:

(1) The use of the telephone to market goods and services to the home and other businesses is now pervasive due to the increased use of cost-effective telemarketing techniques.

(2) Over 30,000 businesses actively telemarket goods and services to business and residential customers.

(3) More than 300,000 solicitors call more than 18,000,000 Americans every day.

(4) Total United States sales generated through telemarketing amounted to $435,000,000,000 in 1990, a more than four-fold increase since 1984.

(5) Unrestricted telemarketing, however, can be an intrusive invasion of privacy and, when an emergency or medical assistance telephone line is seized, a risk to public safety.

(6) Many consumers are outraged over the proliferation of intrusive, nuisance calls to their homes from telemarketers.

(7) Over half the States now have statutes restricting various uses of the telephone for marketing, but telemarketers can evade their prohibitions through interstate operations; therefore, Federal law is needed to control residential telemarketing practices.

(8) The Constitution does not prohibit restrictions on commercial telemarketing solicitations.

(9) Individuals' privacy rights, public safety interests, and commercial freedoms of speech and trade must be balanced in a way that protects the privacy of individuals and permits legitimate telemarketing practices.

(10) Evidence compiled by the Congress indicates that residential telephone subscribers consider automated or prerecorded telephone calls, regardless of the content or the initiator of the message, to be a nuisance and an invasion of privacy.

(11) Technologies that might allow consumers to avoid receiving such calls are not universally available, are costly, are unlikely to be enforced, or place an inordinate burden on the consumer.

(12) Banning such automated or prerecorded telephone calls to the home, except when the receiving party consents to receiving the call or when such calls are necessary in an emergency situation affecting the health and safety of the consumer, is the only effective means of protecting telephone consumers from this nuisance and privacy invasion.

(13) While the evidence presented to the Congress indicates that automated or prerecorded calls are a nuisance and an invasion of privacy, regardless of the type of call, the Federal Communications Commission should have the flexibility to design different rules for those types of automated or prerecorded calls that it finds are not considered a nuisance or invasion of privacy, or for noncommercial calls, consistent with the free speech protections embodied in the First Amendment of the Constitution.

(14) Businesses also have complained to the Congress and the Federal Communications Commission that automated or prerecorded telephone calls are a nuisance, are an invasion of privacy, and interfere with interstate commerce.

(15) The Federal Communications Commission should consider adopting reasonable restrictions on automated or prerecorded calls to businesses as well as to the home, consistent with the constitutional protections of free speech.

47 U.S.C. § 227. Restrictions on use of telephone equipment [abridged]

(a) Definitions

As used in this section—
> (1) The term "automatic telephone dialing system" means equipment which has the capacity—
>> (A) to store or produce telephone numbers to be called, using a random or sequential number generator; and
>> (B) to dial such numbers.
>
> [...]

(4) The term "telephone solicitation" means the initiation of a telephone call or message for the purpose of encouraging the purchase or rental of, or investment in, property, goods, or services, which is transmitted to any person, but such term does not include a call or message (A) to any person with that person's prior express invitation or permission, (B) to any person with whom the caller has an established business relationship, or (C) by a tax exempt nonprofit organization.
(5) The term "unsolicited advertisement" means any material advertising the commercial availability or quality of any property, goods, or services which is transmitted to any person without that person's prior express invitation or permission, in writing or otherwise.

(b) Restrictions on use of automated telephone equipment

(1) Prohibitions

It shall be unlawful for any person within the United States, or any person outside the United States if the recipient is within the United States—

(A) to make any call (other than a call made for emergency purposes or made with the prior express consent of the called party) using any automatic telephone dialing system or an artificial or prerecorded voice—

(i) to any emergency telephone line (including any "911" line and any emergency line of a hospital, medical physician or service office, health care facility, poison control center, or fire protection or law enforcement agency);
(ii) to the telephone line of any guest room or patient room of a hospital, health care facility, elderly home, or similar establishment; or
(iii) to any telephone number assigned to a paging service, cellular telephone service, specialized mobile radio service, or other radio common carrier service, or any service for which the called party is charged for the call;

(B) to initiate any telephone call to any residential telephone line using an artificial or prerecorded voice to deliver a message without the prior express consent of the called party, unless the call is initiated for emergency purposes or is exempted by rule or order by the Commission under paragraph (2)(B);

(C) to use any telephone facsimile machine, computer, or other device to send, to a telephone facsimile machine, an unsolicited advertisement, unless—

> (i) the unsolicited advertisement is from a sender with an established business relationship with the recipient;
>
> (ii) the sender obtained the number of the telephone facsimile machine through—
>
>> (I) the voluntary communication of such number, within the context of such established business relationship, from the recipient of the unsolicited advertisement, or
>>
>> (II) a directory, advertisement, or site on the Internet to which the recipient voluntarily agreed to make available its facsimile number for public distribution,
>
> [...]
>
> (iii) the unsolicited advertisement contains a notice meeting the requirements under paragraph (2)(D), [...]

(D) to use an automatic telephone dialing system in such a way that two or more telephone lines of a multi-line business are engaged simultaneously.

(2) Regulations; exemptions and other provisions

The Commission shall prescribe regulations to implement the requirements of this subsection. In implementing the requirements of this subsection, the Commission—

> (A) shall consider prescribing regulations to allow businesses to avoid receiving calls made using an artificial or prerecorded voice to which they have not given their prior express consent;

(B) may, by rule or order, exempt from the requirements of paragraph (1)(B) of this subsection, subject to such conditions as the Commission may prescribe—
> (i) calls that are not made for a commercial purpose; and
> (ii) such classes or categories of calls made for commercial purposes as the Commission determines—
>> (I) will not adversely affect the privacy rights that this section is intended to protect; and
>> (II) do not include the transmission of any unsolicited advertisement;

(C) may, by rule or order, exempt from the requirements of paragraph (1)(A)(iii) of this subsection calls to a telephone number assigned to a cellular telephone service that are not charged to the called party, subject to such conditions as the Commission may prescribe as necessary in the interest of the privacy rights this section is intended to protect;
[...]

(3) Private right of action

A person or entity may, if otherwise permitted by the laws or rules of court of a State, bring in an appropriate court of that State—
> (A) an action based on a violation of this subsection or the regulations prescribed under this subsection to enjoin such violation,
> (B) an action to recover for actual monetary loss from such a violation, or to receive $500 in damages for each such violation, whichever is greater, or
> (C) both such actions.

If the court finds that the defendant willfully or knowingly violated this subsection or the regulations prescribed under this subsection, the court may, in its discretion, increase the amount of the award to an amount equal to not more than 3 times the amount available under subparagraph (B) of this paragraph.

(c) Protection of subscriber privacy rights

[Paragraphs (1) through (4) authorize the FCC to implement a Do-Not-Call database and enact regulations to enforce it.]

(5) Private right of action

A person who has received more than one telephone call within any 12-month period by or on behalf of the same entity in violation of the regulations prescribed under this subsection may, if otherwise permitted by the laws or rules of court of a State bring in an appropriate court of that State—
    (A) an action based on a violation of the regulations prescribed under this subsection to enjoin such violation,
    (B) an action to recover for actual monetary loss from such a violation, or to receive up to $500 in damages for each such violation, whichever is greater, or
    (C) both such actions.
It shall be an affirmative defense in any action brought under this paragraph that the defendant has established and implemented, with due care, reasonable practices and procedures to effectively prevent telephone solicitations in violation of the regulations prescribed under this subsection. If the court finds that the defendant willfully or knowingly violated the regulations prescribed under this subsection, the court may, in its discretion, increase the amount of the award to an amount equal to not more than 3 times the amount available under subparagraph (B) of this paragraph.

[...]

(d) Technical and procedural standards

[...]

(3) Artificial or prerecorded voice systems

The Commission shall prescribe technical and procedural standards for systems that are used to transmit any artificial or prerecorded voice message via telephone. Such standards shall require that—

(A) all artificial or prerecorded telephone messages (i) shall, at the beginning of the message, state clearly the identity of the business, individual, or other entity initiating the call, and (ii) shall, during or after the message, state clearly the telephone number or address of such business, other entity, or individual; and
(B) any such system will automatically release the called party's line within 5 seconds of the time notification is transmitted to the system that the called party has hung up, to allow the called party's line to be used to make or receive other calls.

(e) Prohibition on provision of inaccurate caller identification information

(1) In general

It shall be unlawful for any person within the United States, in connection with any telecommunications service or IP-enabled voice service, to cause any caller identification service to knowingly transmit misleading or inaccurate caller identification information with the intent to defraud, cause harm, or wrongfully obtain anything of value, unless such transmission is exempted pursuant to paragraph (3)(B).

[...]

(f) Effect on State law

(1) State law not preempted

Except for the standards prescribed under subsection (d) of this section and subject to paragraph (2) of this subsection, nothing in this section or in the regulations prescribed under this section shall preempt any State law that imposes more restrictive intrastate requirements or regulations on, or which prohibits—
(A) the use of telephone facsimile machines or other electronic devices to send unsolicited advertisements;
(B) the use of automatic telephone dialing systems;

(C) the use of artificial or prerecorded voice messages; or
(D) the making of telephone solicitations.

[...]

(g) Actions by States

[...]

(h) Junk fax enforcement report

[...]

www.ingramcontent.com/pod-product-compliance
Lightning Source LLC
Chambersburg PA
CBHW072028230526
45466CB00020B/1098